VISION DUBAI 2022: REALISING THE DREAM

Nazimudeen Saleem

Armahn Books

Completed in July 2016

C@ N Saleem

Copyright ©2016 All rights reserved

No part of this publication may be reproduced, stored in a retrieval system, or transmitted, in any form or by any means, without the prior permission in writing of the publisher, not be otherwise circulated in any form of binding or cover other than that in which it is published and without a similar condition including this condition being imposed on the subsequent purchaser.

The moral right of Nazimudeen Saleem is asserted.

Acknowledgement:

The author would like to acknowledge the moral support and enthusiasm shown by Dr Husam Awadalla when writing this book. He also provided the cover picture. I would like to thank my wife for her patience.

Createspace Charleston SC

Author/publisher: Nazimudeen Saleem 2016

Dedicated to the ruler of Dubai:
His Highness Sheikh Mohammed Bin Rashid Al Maktoum
The Vice President and the Prime Minister of the UAE

Preface

Since the late 1990s, Dubai, with its liberal outlook and business friendly environment, had attracted foreign investors not only for the exploitation of its petroleum resources but also to engage in business and economic development. Recently, Dubai has been scoring high on political and economic stability index. As a visionary and strategist, the ruler of Dubai has been personally involved in making his city-state a wonderful and cherished destination to live and work for everyone.

With the hosting of Expo 2020, Dubai has its vision beyond 2020. The emirate sees its future in non-petroleum sectors such as leisure and tourism where shopping and entertainment along with beach-driven activities will remain important. Moreover, its offshore strategy, particularly in the banking and finance sector, is also said to dominate. The Emirate of Dubai is embracing a visitor cum knowledge-led service economy.

In the meantime, the global economic environment is rather turbulent and gloomy. The uncertainty caused by Brexit, the US presidential election, falling oil and commodity prices, and the stagnating economies of the West are all causes for concern.

The ageing economies in the West, including the Japanese, are suffering from a chronic illness inflicted by an unsustainable level of sovereign debt and fiscal deficit while the unsustainable level of falling oil price is hurting the oil-dependent economies of the Gulf States and other countries such as Russia, Nigeria and Venezuela.

Even with the extraordinary measures taken by the Central Banks, economic recovery in the West seems still far away. Even with plenty of cheap money available for lending, the West is struggling to cope up with its previous national and consumer debts. Unexpected fall in oil price since the late 2015s has also affected the oil-exporting economies of the GCC and the unsustainable level of fiscal deficits are causing shockwaves in these countries.

Dubai as well as the UAE has also been affected badly and this could affect the ongoing development and construction projects. According to emirates247.com, the total value of construction projects currently underway in Dubai is estimated to be $53.6 billion. And, those under planning are valued at $337.2 billion or Dh1.23 trillion. Even the GDP growth of Dubai is expected to be lower in 2016 than the previous years.

As the economic climate continues to deteriorate, the author is concerned about its consequences on the future development projects in Dubai. You may wonder if the vision 2020 and beyond would remain a dream or can be realised as planned.

The economies of the West were already crippled with a mountain of sovereign debt even before the crisis. Widening fiscal deficit and a growing current account deficit further augment the problem. These economies could not recover from the post-crisis paralysis yet and no one seems to have any answers.

The crisis had even crippled Dubai which felt the tremor in 2009. With the blessing of the rising oil price, the emirate did recover gradually but to face another crisis again in 2015 when the oil price started to bleed again to reach the abys in January 2016.

With a widening fiscal deficit, the oil-dependent economies, including the Emirates and Dubai are being forced to slash their current spending, including those allocated for major projects. Although Dubai is less dependent on oil export, its economy could suffer from plunging oil prices and falling tourism revenue as the depressed economies of the West suffer from austerity measures.

However, the ruler of Dubai HH Sheikh Mohammed Bin Rashid Al Maktoum is committed to realizing his vision. And, the emirate has its future development strategy firmly on the ground. Although the ongoing global economic slowdown could shed some doubts on its success, the Dubai strategy is being implemented ostensibly. Financial sustainability however remains questionable and therefore requires prudent but unconventional economic and financial management strategies.

In overall, the key question is whether the debt-financed economic model based on western capitalism could survive in the long-run. The author's 'sovereign equity' concept is proposed here as an alternative to the sovereign debt model. The author is convinced that this model can be applied effectively to a modern well-managed state like Dubai which has all the necessary institutional infrastructure and organisational framework for successful adoption. The application of the sovereign equity model enables the nation-state to manage its economy effectively along with other appropriate fiscal measures to become totally debt-free. A debt-free and interest-free economy at the sovereign level not only makes it sustainable but also aligns with the Islamic principles.

This brief book is dedicated to the ruler of Dubai HH Sheikh Mohammed Bin Rashid Al Maktoum who has his firm vision for the emirate. The proposed model should help realise his dream while attaining sustainable economic development and prosperity within the Islamic framework.

Nazimudeen Saleem
London
21 July 2016

VIII

VISION DUBAI 2022: REALISING THE DREAM

CONTENTS

1. VISION DUBAI 2022: REALISING THE DREAM
   An Introduction 7

2. HISTORIC EVOLUTION OF THE UAE AS A NATION

   The Trucial Rulers and the Sheikdoms 15

   The United Arab Emirates 16

   Oiling the UAE Economy 18
   Emirate of Dubai 21

3. TWENTY-FIRST CENTURY DUBAI

   A Modern City-State 27

   Future of Dubai: Visitor cum Knowledge-led Service Economy 29
   A Blueprint for a Smart City 34

4. DUBAI AND THE EMERGING GLOBAL ECONOMIC TRENDS

   The West and the Global Economic Crisis 51

   Impacts of Globalisation 55

   Sovereign Debt Crisis 59

   The End of Western Economic Hegemony 64
   The Global Economic Trends Affecting Dubai 69

5. A BLUEPRINT FOR A DEBT-FREE SUSTAINABLE ECONOMY

   Rational for a Debt-free Sustainable Economy 83

   Sovereign Debt versus Sovereign Equity 88

   Fiscal Policy Measures and Taxation 95
   Sovereign Equity Fund and the Sovereign Holding Corporation 102

1. VISION DUBAI 2022: REALISING THE DREAM

An Introduction

1. VISION DUBAI 2022: REALISING THE DREAM

An Introduction

The small emirate of Dubai in the Arabian coast of the Persian Gulf outshines all the other countries in the Middle East in every sense. Whether on the global competitive index or political and economic stability score, the emirate of Dubai has established itself a niche within a period of just 20 years. The ruler of Dubai has been and still is a visionary who has courageously pursued and meticulously implemented an economic development strategy which has paved the way for the recent success.

The ruler already has a vision for 2020. With the scheduled Expo 2020, Dubai tries to excel what the emirate has achieved so far with an economic diversification strategy. It means, Dubai sees the future in non-petroleum sectors and the main emphasis is on leisure and tourism where shopping and entertainment along with beach-driven activities will remain important. In addition, offshore banking and finance sector is also said to have taken off. In this regard, the visitors to Dubai are expected to be leisure tourists as well as business travellers. The Emirate of Dubai tends to be a visitor cum knowledge-led service economy.

The global economic environment, however, is rather shaky and uncertainty is rife, particularly in the already ageing economies of the West. Unexpectedly, it also affects the oil-dependent economies of the Middle East. The pioneering economies of the West, including Japanese, are suffering from a chronic illness inflicted by an unsustainable level of sovereign debt and widening fiscal deficit for sometimes. In other words, economic superiority of the West is coming to an end. In the meantime, falling oil price is hurting the oil-dependent economies of the Gulf States along with other countries such as Russia, Nigeria and Venezuela to mention a few. Over-production of oil and the shale gas exploitation in the USA and elsewhere is causing the oil and gas prices to decline beyond expectation.

The future economic environment, although difficult to predict, seems bleak and the current climate indicates that nothing is going to change. The Central Bankers all over the world wonder why all the measures implemented since the financial crisis fail to yield any positive outcomes. This would definitely have negative impacts on the several West-dependent economies such as the United Arab Emirates or any other Gulf States.

When an economy cannot generate the projected revenue due to external forces such as the falling oil price, the fiscal deficit would widen to an unmanageable level as in Saudi Arabia or Russia which would lead to abandoning several cherished development projects. This also seems to be true with the UAE and Dubai.

According to a recent report (1) on the construction sector in Dubai, the total value of projects under construction in the Emirate is estimated to be $53.6 billion and the projects under planning are valued at $337.2 billion or Dh1.23 trillion. The report says the majority of the current or planned developments are in the residential sector which is estimated to be $66.4 billion. However, recent government statistics show the slowing phase of GDP growth in Dubai during 2015 when compared to the previous years of 2014 and 2013.

The author is concerned that the current economic climate would also impact the future development projects of the gulf emirates, particularly Dubai. One may wonder if the vision Dubai 2020 would remain a dream or can anything be done to realise the ruler's vision.

The debt-financed economies of the West and Japan enjoyed their growth to maturity during the last fifty or so years reaching the climax in the 1990s and to some extent in the early 2000s. When the tsunami of credit crunch and the financial crisis hit the West, particularly the USA, policy makers and the economists failed to realise that it was not the usual recession or economic stagnation but a symptom of a chronic illness.

The Western economies were crippled with a huge and growing problem of sovereign debt, persistent and widening fiscal deficit, and an uncontrollable level of negative trade balance or current account deficit. Government debt, corporate debt and consumer debt all have hit their climax during this period and touched ground in the late 2007s to the early 2008s with an unexpected squeeze in the credit level leading to the financial and banking crisis.

The West could not recover from this post-crisis paralysis yet and the economists and the policy makers haven't got any answers. The crisis had spread like a wildfire and even the Emirate of Dubai felt the tremor in 2009. Thanks to the hiking oil price during the post-crisis period, the oil-dependent economies recovered gradually. That was until 2015 when the world oil market began to bleed with over supply.

A barrel of oil hit the lowest since 2005 in January 2016 reaching $27 US which would suddenly plunge the revenue of oil-dependent economies such as Saudi Arabia, Russia, and even the Gulf States and bring them to their knees. While commodity prices may go up and down with some negative impacts on the dependent economies, consequence of plunging oil price could not be anything pleasant. What is worst is its unavoidable link to the global economic environment which is very much depended on debt financed public and fiscal spending as well as consumer spending.

Strangely enough the policy makers and central bankers have tried all what they have learned and practiced to remedy the economic malaise but none has proven to be successful even with negative interest rates and frequent doses of 'quantitative easing' to print money at the mercy of inflation. While the Western economies have been taking austerity measures for sometimes along with other failed economic policies adopted, oil-dependent states are forced to slash their current budget in order to balance their books. It is hurting them unprecedentedly.

Although the emirate of Dubai is less dependent on oil export, and its economy is to some extent diversified, it can suffer from a double blow of plunging oil price and a fall in tourism revenue due to depressed economies of the West and their austerity measures. In fact, implementing Dubai's visitor-led economic development strategy may be in jeopardy. This is because the tourism producing countries in the West as well as the other oil-dependent economies of the Gulf are facing economic slowdown.

The real issue here is the sustainability of a credit-led debt-financed economic model. Credit is a commodity invented by the capitalist bankers and it has done a marvellous job in the conception and development of the Western economic model. Today, however, its over-consumption has created an addictive economic illness that we find it difficult to recover or escape from. The author wonders whether an alternative model that is akin to Islamic finance model based on 'sovereign equity' rather than sovereign debt could be the answer.

According to the proposed model, a nation-state economy can conceive its own public equity called 'sovereign equity' while also generating revenue from appropriate fiscal measures in order to function totally debt-free. Although most nation-states may find it difficult to implement this concept due to practical reasons which would become clear later, a modern well-structured and organised small states such as Singapore or Dubai would find it attractive and workable. After all, a debt-free and interest-free economy is a sustainable economy which is the key to making a smart economy without which a state or city cannot become smart either.

The 'Sovereign Equity' model of economic management offers two key benefits. It helps generate additional income or revenue for the state and minimise the need for borrowing. Also, it offers the participant stakeholders of the economy, who are the tax-payer citizens, an opportunity to become shareholders of the economy.

A debt-free as well as interest-free economy at the nation-state level not only aligns with the Islamic principles but also provides sustainability. It is obvious that up until now, Islamic principles have been applied to consumer and corporate related banking and finance products and not related to nation-state finances or at the State Treasury level, except the sukuk bonds. Even the Islamic states that promote and practice Islamic banking and finance still depend on the traditional debt instruments such as the bonds and other similar products all of which carry interest payments when they borrow money.

The emirate of Dubai itself is an example which requires borrowing from the market using traditional methods directly or indirectly to finance its ambitious economic development projects. Adoption of an economic management system based on the proposed sovereign equity model can lead the way for a totally debt-free financing when applied along with appropriate fiscal policy tools to fund the development projects.

The author strongly believes that an efficient state like Dubai and Singapore as well as other small well-managed nations can easily adopt the concept of sovereign equity along with a few relevant fiscal policy instruments to effectively manage their economies. This is because these modern and efficient states already have the framework and structure as well as the organisational profile that would easily fit the criteria for implementing the proposed model.

It does not, however, mean that the proposed model cannot be implemented elsewhere. Adoption of the sovereign equity model by the debt-ridden nations in the West definitely would pave the way for a debt-free economy.

In this brief book, the author has chosen the emirate of Dubai to examine the application of the sovereign equity concept as its ruler HH Sheikh Mohammed Bin Rashid Al Maktoum has been ambitiously pursuing a grandiose plan for his city-state. Being a modern and efficient state, the Dubai has the necessary institutional infrastructure and the organisational structure to enable the adoption of the proposed model relatively easily.

Moreover, the emirate of Dubai has its future economic development plan firmly on the ground and it is being implemented although the unexpected global economic malaise almost seems to affects its smooth take off and operations.

As the title of this book implies, Dubai already has a vision, and the proposed model, as the author believes, should help realise the ruler's dream while enabling the emirate to achieve sustainable economic growth within the Islamic framework.

The rest of the book is arranged in four short chapters with the second chapter outlining the historic evolution of the emirates. The third and the fourth chapters examine the modern Dubai and its future as well as the factors affecting the implementation of the future plan along with the expected roadblocks. The fifth chapter explains the concept of sovereign equity and its application in the management of economy. This chapter also examines how Dubai can overcome the barriers by adopting the proposed concept in order to realise its vision 2022.

2. HISTORIC EVOLUTION OF THE UAE AS A NATION

The Trucial Rulers and the Sheikdoms

The United Arab Emirates

Oiling the UAE Economy

Emirate of Dubai

2. HISTORIC EVOLUTION OF THE UAE AS A NATION

The Trucial Rulers and the Sheikdoms

The United Arab Emirates (UAE) is a nation of seven small sheikdoms called the emirates that lies in the North-eastern shores of the Arabian Peninsula in the Persian Gulf.

The UAE came to existence as a federation of six emirates on December 2, 1971. The largest of the federation Abu Dhabi along with Dubai, Sharjah, Ajman, Umm Al Quwain and Fujairah first joined together to form the union and later on February 10, 1972, the seventh sheikdom Ras Al Khaimah joined the federation. These seven sheikhdoms were previously called the Trucial States based on a treaty made in the 19th Century by the Trucial sheikhs with the British (2).

In the fifteen-hundreds, most parts of the Gulf's coastal region were under the control of the Ottomans (3) until the Portuguese on their way to the east made intrusion. The Portuguese is said to have controlled the Arabian Peninsula for over 150 years (3). The early Portuguese seafarers occupied the coastal areas on their way to the far-east during the fifteenth century, but with resistance and skirmishes from local inhabitants headed by Trucial Sheikhs. The Ottomans, however, regained control of the region until the fall of the empire after the First World War when the Trucial States became British protectorates.

Archaeological discoveries in the region testify its historic trade link with the surrounding regions that stretches as far as modern day Syria. The peninsula was believed to have been inhabited by a number of Bedouin tribes later to settle in the coastal areas after the arrival of Islam in the six-hundreds.

The coastal areas controlled by the Trucial Sheikhs of the peninsula remained a threat to the seafarers, including the British who were on their pursuit of Indian Ocean expansion strategy. In order to protect the Indian trade route, British singed several treaties with the sheikhs. The British recognition of the Trucial States, in fact, created a pocket of sheikdoms in the region.

After British gaining control of the area later in the nineteenth century and signing of the treaty with the Trucial leaders in 1850s, there seemed to have been some peace and stability in the region (4). In 1982, the Trucial sheikhs singed a treaty with the British to protect their land from other foreign invaders (5). During the period of relative calm and peace in the region under the protection of the British, pearling flourished. Fishing and pearl diving remained the key economic activities but the collapse of the pearl trade in 1930 brought about hardship to the inhabitants of the coastal areas.

In 1968, the British decided to leave the region and withdrew from its involvement in the Trucial states that led to the creation of the federation. The federation treaty was agreed by the ruler of Abu Dhabi, Sheikh Zayed bin Sultan Al Nahyan and the ruler of Dubai, Sheikh Rashid bin Saeed Al Maktoum. Later, other Trucial rulers joined the federation to form the United Arab Emirates in 1971.

The United Arab Emirates

The United Arab Emirates today is a modern country with a well-developed infrastructure and diversified economy. The emirate of Dubai is a highly developed city-state which is developing into a global hub for tourism, retail, and finance (6). Dubai is also home to the world's tallest building and the largest man-made seaport. Some 80% of the UAE population is non-citizen and virtually all citizens of the country or Emiratis are Muslims. The rulers of both Abu Dhabi and Dubai belong to the Sunni sect and follow the Maliki traditions of Islam (sheikhmohammed.com/ae).

While the ruler of Abu Dhabi is the President of the federation, the ruler of Dubai remains the Vice President and the Prime

Minister. The Prime Minister and Vice President, HH Sheikh Mohammed bin Rashid Al Maktoum, in his website portrays himself as a leader, father, poet and a knight. He quotes 'The record of the UAE's economy bears testament to the wise vision of the country's leadership and the sound legislation that guarantees the stability of all investments in various sectors'. Recently, HH Shaikh Mohammed bin Rashid has set social media record for the most engaging political leader with a LinkedIn post on 27 February 2016. It was about his rationale for establishing cabinet ministries for happiness, tolerance, youth and future.

The United Arab Emirates is a federation of seven sheikdoms or emirates and it is governed by a Federal Supreme Council consisting of hereditary monarchs or the seven emirs. The Supreme Council elects the President and the Prime Minister. At present, the ruler of Abu Dhabi holds the Presidency while the ruler of Dubai holds the Prime Minister post. As a tradition, the Prime Minister is also holds the post of the Vice President.

The governmental responsibilities are shared between the national government and the emirates (7). Each emirate has its revenue generating power but a percentage of revenues from each contribute to the national budget of the federation (8). The day-to-day affairs of the nation are supervised by the Federal National Council (FNC). It consists of forty members where half of them are elected to serve the nation for a period of two years. The other half is appointed by the rulers of the seven emirates. The FNC currently enjoys limited authority and its role is essentially consultative in nature (9). The UAE has an effective platform for e-Government which is considered an extension to the national government. So is the case of Dubai where e-portal with a facility for over 40 services is considered very effective.

The citizens and the residents enjoy substantial freedom in the UAE compared to other monarchical regimes in the Middle East although it is seen as an autocracy by the Western world. The seven hereditary monarchical rulers adopt an independent approach to controlling their own territorial integrity and they seem to have a distinct vision for each emirate following the already celebrated Dubai. Abu Dhabi with its largest land area of the union and thus its resources, including oil, is said to taken off aggressively recently. The city of Abu Dhabi as the capital of the UAE is poised to grow with its own vision.

The UAE as a federation, however, is very much integrated and the federal government is determined to develop the nation strategically with a modern infrastructure as well as supra-structure. The UAE currently has three international airports with another modern airport under development in Dubai. Dubai International and Abu Dhabi International airports are among the busiest in the region with two national airlines as flag carriers, Emirates Airlines and Etihad Airlines operating from the UAE.

Oiling the UAE Economy

According to the US Energy Information Agency (10), the UAE is among the largest 10 oil producers in the world. The UAE is both a member of the Organization of the Petroleum Exporting Countries (OPEC) and the Gas Exporting Countries Forum (GECF). The country's oil reserves are one of the largest in the Middle East and estimated to be nearly 100 billion barrels.

The Oil & Gas Journal estimates that the UAE holds the seventh-largest proven reserves of oil in the world at 97.8 billion barrels in 2015 but over 90% of the reserves are said to be in the emirate of Abu Dhabi with the rest spread among other emirates (11).

Dubai's reserves are estimated to be just 4 billion barrels. Today, the UAE is a major oil producer as well as an exporter. The latest figures show that the country produced an average of 3.5 million barrels per day of petroleum and other liquids in 2014. According to the IMF sources, hydrocarbon exports generated revenue of $123 billion for the country in 2013.

The UAE was the second-largest producer of petroleum and other liquids in OPEC ranking them second in petroleum production in the OPEC behind Saudi Arabia. The UAE was the fourth-largest crude oil producer in OPEC in 2014. The country plans to increase crude oil production to 3.5 million barrels a day in 2020 essentially with Enhanced Oil Recovery (EOR) techniques applied in the existing oil fields as the prospects for further discoveries are limited. However, achieving this target seems doubtful if the oil price stays low below $50 a barrel.

The oil industry in the UAE is regulated by each of the seven emirates within their borders. Each emirate is responsible for regulating the oil industry within its borders but production-sharing strategy does offers synergy to some extent. The Supreme Petroleum Council (SPC) formulates and implements petroleum-related policies in Abu Dhabi and the emirate as the major producer; the SPC plays an important role for the entire country. The SPC implements its policies through the Abu Dhabi National Oil Company (ADNOC) which is responsible for the day-to-day operations, including oil and gas exploration through its subsidiaries. In the meantime, Supreme Council of Energy (DSCE) is responsible for Dubai's energy policy formulation and supervision. The DSCE integrates all responsible authorities from various energy related agencies in order to ensure that Dubai has adequate measures to respond to the future energy needs. The discovery and export of oil in the late 1950s and early 1960s did, in fact, provided the resources and foundation for the development of Abu Dhabi.

Today, Abu Dhabi city as the capital of the UAE is a modern city with a diversified economy and a million inhabitants. It was a sparsely populated small city when Sheikh Zayed bin Sultan Al Nahyan became the ruler in 1966. But the oil revenue has changed everything; high-rise buildings with boulevard-like streets, and man-made gardens. Although the country has been a late starter in terms of drilling and oil exports, the oil industry is well-structured and managed. The UAE enjoys a good standard of living with efficient and adequate public services provisions.

The UAE has already started its economic diversification strategy and Dubai is in its Centre; it has become one of the leading financial and trading centers in the Middle East. Foreign Direct Investments in the country and, particularly in Dubai has increased in the past. Investment in other industrial sectors such as leisure and hospitality as well as real estate, technology, and media and shopping ensure the UAE will remain economically sustainable.

However, in the current global economic climate, sustaining economic growth is a real challenge. Although the real GDP of the UAE seems to be growing at 5.2% in 2013 (12) which is more than the growth rates of the Western economies, there is a real danger whether the growth can be sustained if the current oil price continues to slide and the Western economies continue to slowdown.

Moreover, domestic consumption of oil and gas is also rising. The UAE is an exporter as well as an importer of liquefied natural gas and the US EIA data (13) shows that the country is today a net importer of natural gas since 2008. With the growing demand for electricity which is generated from natural gas fired facilities and the use of EOR process, which helps to boost oil production, the UAE is trying to meet the current domestic demand from imports. The country may continue to import gas for sometimes in the future. This is in addition to boosting natural gas production from other unexploited gas deposits, as the country still seems to depend very much on the export of petroleum related products.

The UAE is currently seeking alternative energy resources in order to meet its growing demand sustainably. It is adding nuclear and renewable energy generating facilities along with coal-fired electricity generating capacity. However, it relies heavily on natural gas at the moment as current economic development projects and population growth continues which triggers further growth in the electricity consumption. When the price of oil and gas fall, it would become cheaper to import rather than depend on domestic production in the near future. It is worth noting that the UAE stands among the countries of highest per capita electricity consumption in the world. According to a report in the Gulf News, demand for electricity in the UAE could even grow, 50% by 2020 (14).

The Emirate of Dubai

According to the historical data in record, Dubai had not seen the oil revenue coming in until 1970s but the flowing oil revenue since the 1980s did help develop Dubai as a Global City and a trading hub within a period of a few decades. It was during the late 1990s and early 2000s that Dubai emerged as one of the leading business and trading centres connecting the Middle East, Asia and the African continent.

Today Dubai remains a major transport hub for both passengers and cargo. Dubai as an emirate is much smaller than Abu Dhabi and its oil reserves are however limited. Unlike its cousin, Abu Dhabi, Dubai had to or forced to diversify its economy.

The city-state is one of the westernised enclaves among the Gulf States and now its economy is driven by revenues coming from leisure and hospitality, trading, banking and financial services, aviation, and real estate. Dubai has become a destination brand name today for leisure and business visitors attracting millions of travellers for sports, tourism, shopping, conference, exhibitions, as well as for business.

The Dubai city is also famous for its city landscape consisting of Manhattan-like clusters of tall but modern buildings nested with ultra-modern infrastructure and well-maintained parks. There are several iconic buildings and skyscrapers in Dubai today. The world's tallest tower, the Burj Khalifa is a marvelous work of architecture in its own right. Recently, Dubai has been successfully sponsoring a number of sports, business and leisure events too.

The emirate did however experience a shocking tremor during the recent global financial crisis and the property market in Dubai almost did collapse in 2009. Surprisingly, Dubai withstood and recovered gradually. Today, Dubai may be one of the most expensive cities in the Middle East and one of the expensive cities in the world for both the residents and visitors but visitor numbers to the city is still on the rise.

The Dubai Municipality (DM) or city government works with the government of Dubai but it is a separate entity with a designated budget. The DM which was created by the former ruler of Dubai has been instrumental in the planning and development of the city from the beginning. Dubai Municipality is responsible for the urban development planning, provision of public services and the maintenance of the city's facilities.

Through its various departments such as planning, roads, sewage, environment and public health, and finance, the DM operates like any similar municipalities in the West. The DM has successfully launched an ambitious e-Government project which seems to be functioning well by providing a number of key services through its web portal.

The area around the Dubai Creek remains the Centre of the city which cut across the northeast and southwest of the emirate. Today, it is rather a congested urban area but acts as the nerve Centre of Dubai. For an outsider, this is where the real Dubai to be seen with the flourishing real estate developments in the east of the creek, and further along the coast of Jumeirah. Even the Business Bay along with Port Rashid and Jebel Ali are also located here. Other key attractions to be seen in the area are Burj Al Arab, the Palm Jumeirah and the theme-based free-zone.

The old part of the city with new development taking place is the western area of Deira where the Dubai International Airport (DIA) is situated. The DIA opened in 1960, now serves some seventy million passengers and which is expected to reach 100 million before the end of the decade.

In 2015, flights from and to the DIA reached 260 destinations. Its purpose built facilities include A380 concourse and the expected renovation and expansion project at a cost of 7.8 billion US with the expansion of Terminal 2 is scheduled to complete in 2020 (15). Dubai is full of foreigners where over 80% of the residents belong to the expatriate community. The majority of expatriates are Asian, mainly from the Indians Subcontinent. Over one hundred thousand British expatriates make the largest among the non-Asians living in Dubai. English is the widely spoken language in Dubai because the UAE as a whole and, Dubai in particular, is run by mainly English speaking expatriates. In Dubai, only 10 to 15 percent of the population is accounted for the UAE nationals.

The population density of Dubai is one of the highest among modern cities around the world. Most non-nationals working in Dubai in the lower paid jobs are living outside Dubai such as in the border-towns of Sharjah and Abu Dhabi. Almost ninety-nine percent of the UAE Arabs are Muslims and Islam is the official religion of the country. The government of Dubai is responsible for managing the mosques and the Imams are appointed by the government. Dubai does not tolerate any Islamic extremism.

Although the UAE is an Islamic country, Dubai's jurisprudence is not totally Islamic. Dubai is not part of the UAE's federal judicial system. It judicial systems follow a quasi-western model and judicial courts consists of the Court of First Instance, the Court of Appeal, and the Court of Cassation. The Court of First Instance hears all civil claims, criminal claims coming from police complaints and other matters and complaints between Muslims under a number of different courts such as the Civil Court, the Criminal Court or Sharia Court. The Court of Cassation acts like the supreme court of Dubai.

3. TWENTY-FIRST CENTURY DUBAI

A Modern City-State

Future of Dubai: Visitor cum Knowledge-led Service Economy

A Blueprint for a Smart City

3. TWENTY-FIRST CENTURY DUBAI

A Modern City-State

Within the UAE, Dubai City is a unique place. For some, the whole of Dubai would seem like an amusement park but for others, it can resemble Manhattan in New York. For another group of people, Dubai could seem to be the place for shopping. Obviously, Dubai hosts the tallest tower along with several other tall buildings to lighten up the city-scape.

The Dubai city also remains the host to some of the most expensive hotels in the world. Whatever it is, Dubai wouldn't have evolved to become a modern city without the vision, strategy and determination of its ruler HH Sheikh Mohammed bin Rashid Al Maktoum.

Today, Dubai as a city has grown to include its periphery although it first emerged around Dubai Creek. The south side of the Dubai Creek, Deira has become an integral part of Dubai City now but in the earlier days, it remained an independent city in the south. The new Dubai city in the northern section of the creek has become almost unrecognisable today.

In the development of Dubai as a city, Bur Dubai in the north of Dubai Creek has played a vital role. This is where everything started, paving the way for the economic boon in the later years. The community around the creek and its souks and trading activities all had the foundation historically.

Today, the Dubai Creek Park remains a tourist attraction with boutiques and jewellery shops. Moreover, most of the modern business centers as well as banking and financial centers are headquartered here which is near to the port area. In the earlier days, Dubai was also famous for free trade in gold until 1990s. After the construction of the largest man-made port, Jebel Ali, some forty years ago, Dubai quickly became an active trading Centre. The export of petroleum products and import of consumer goods played an important role in this regard.

Today, Dubai is also a Centre for key service sector businesses, including media, Information & Communication Technology, and finance. Dubai also boasts several industry specific Free Zones where several multinationals corporations have their businesses as well as head offices situated.

Dubai is a crammed city although ultra-modern with state-of-the-art infrastructure supported by technology. Adoption of modern technology plays an important role in administering and managing the modern city of Dubai. Whether it is the provision of public services or delivering essential services through the private sector companies, Dubai has got everything in place.

The Dubai hosts a raft of specialist cities such as the Media City, Sports City, Garden City, Health Care City (with state-of-the-art equipment and advanced technology), Finance & Investment Park, Academic City for education related businesses, and Dubai Marina. Dubai has an efficient public transit system with a metro system, trams, buses, waterway transit, and monorail.

Telecommunication in Dubai is still a regulated sector to some extent which would restrict the development the ICT provision and related businesses. Internet content in the UAE as well as in Dubai is regulated and the rulers fear that it would violates the cultural sensitivities of the nation. Moreover, the rulers also believe the uncensored Internet contents could destabilise political structure of the Emirates.

The traditional Islamic values need to be preserved and protected, the government believes. Although the penal code prohibits digital access to certain censored materials such as pornography, Dubai still needs to work on the issues of data protection or cybercrime. Moreover, with all the modernity, the city does have a weakness in terms of its earlier sewage systems in some parts of Dubai. There has been a lot of improvement recently and Dubai has two large waste treatment plants with several smaller ones operating in the emirate. Efficient pumping systems and fast treatment methods also help alleviate the problem today. The Dubai Municipality should also consider enforcing to installing onsite treatment plants with modern technology for some of the clusters of development to further alleviate the problems.

Managing the water supply and demand is also another issue for Dubai. The main source of clean water, including portable water in Dubai is the ocean and is obtained from desalination of sea water using the most efficient desalination plants which use reverse osmosis process. After desalination, water is filtered, treated and mineral salts added to make it fit for human consumption as well as for other household or industrial use.

The cost of desalination is much lower than transporting water from natural sources to the consuming places today. Dubai along with the UAE is committed to managing the water resources sustainably as the country has one of the highest per capita water consumption rates in the world. The Dubai Municipality already uses recycled water for watering the green spaces and parks and encourages the residents to use tap water for drinking.

Future of Dubai: Visitor cum Knowledge-led Service Economy

Growth in visitor traffic based on tourism is extremely important to Dubai and it is an important element of the government's strategy to generate economic activity and to increase the flow of foreign cash into the country. First, the love affair of tourists with Dubai started mainly with shopping. Dubai is claimed to be the 'shopping capital of the Middle East' with several shopping malls.

The city boasts the world largest shopping mall called the Dubai Mall along with other popular centers like the Mall of the Emirates, Deira City Centre, Mirdiff City Centre, Bur Juman, and Ibn Battuta Mall etc. There are several traditional souks, including the famous Gold Souk in Dubai which attracts thousands of visitors from Asia and the Middle East.

Recently, the emirates started to promote it heritage attractions to visitors along with the man-made modern attractions such as the tallest tower in the world, Burj Khalifa and the iconic Burj Al Arab. Among the several other visitor attractions are Palm Jumeirah, Medinat Jumeirah, Palm Islands, Dubai Creek Park, Miracle Garden, Wild Wadi Water Park, and several beach parks such as the Jumeirah Beach Park or Al Mamzar Beach Park. The most tourists also enjoy Desert Safari, Dhow Cruise, sandboarding, balloon flight or a visit to the Al Ain Oasis.

According to the Council on Tall Buildings and Urban Habitat (CTBUH), another new attraction would be the proposed; a 325-metre base-jump tower which would provide a platform for sports activities, including of extreme nature. Moreover, Dubai is famous for its international festivals such as the Dubai Food Festival which is held in February-March every year, Dubai Shopping Festival which is held in January-February, and the Dubai Summer Surprise (DSS) thereafter etc. In the meantime, the emirate also attracts visitors in thousands to view or participate in a number of sports and recreation related events every year. Dubai has a designated Sports City and hosts a number of sports events that attract world attention. The annual Tennis Championship, the Legends Rock tennis tournaments, the Dubai Desert Classic golf tournament and the Dubai World Championship are among the popular events that attract visitors.

Also, the emirate holds a thoroughbred horse race called the Dubai World Cup annually. Other world sports events include the traditional Rugby Union tournament Dubai Sevens and the Fun Ride cycling event as well as many auto racing events every year. In addition, like football, cricket is considered a sort of national sport and the city is the Centre for international cricket events throughout the year. Dubai is also committed to help improve the standard of cricket worldwide with its ICC Cricket Academy, which is the training and coaching school for aspiring young cricketers.

In terms of the visitor traffic, some would claim that Dubai stands within the 10 most visited city in the world, and in 2015 Dubai was expected to host over 15 million tourists. By 2020, Dubai expects the visitor number to go up to 25 million when the EXPO 2020 is scheduled to take place.

When the Expo committee, the delegation from the Bureau International des Expositions, visited to check the readiness and commitment of Dubai in February 2013, they were very much impressed. The Master Plan for Dubai Expo 2020 was presented right away and won the right in November 2013 to host the Expo 2020. The event is expected to bring in huge economic benefits, including the creation of hundreds of thousands of jobs. A 438-hectare site has been chosen within the new Dubai Trade Centre for the Expo.

The future of Dubai very much depends on the new strategy for economic diversification as noted above. Apart from the commodity trade and import and export of manufactured goods as well as retailing, the future will focus on the services such as banking and finance, health care, education, media, and travel and tourism based activities such as events, hospitality and entertainment as well as shopping. Dubai as an economic entity, it depends very much on international trade. In 2014, Dubai's non-oil foreign trade stood at $362 billion (16).

According to the government sources, China, India, the USA, and Saudi Arabia remained the largest trading partners while the countries of the Gulf Cooperation Council, Germany, Switzerland, Japan and the UK were other key trading partners of the emirate in 2014. In terms of the overall trade volume, Dubai seems to import more than it exports but the emirates also re-export large amounts of goods which it imports.

The Emirate of Dubai as well as the UAE rank among the few most developed countries in the region. However, the UAE as a whole still depends on commodity export. Oil and natural gas accounts for nearly 40 percent of the exports as well as in total economic output as measured in GDP. From the beginning of this century, the UAE as well as Dubai in particular, has been making a huge effort to achieve economic diversification in order to reduce its dependence on oil revenues.

An enormous investment has been pumped in Dubai as well as in the UAE in order to diversify the economy into such sectors as tourism, finance and banking and construction.

In the year 2015, Dubai was still growing but at a slower phase than the previous years. The Dubai Statistic Centre (DSC) reports that emirate of Dubai grew by 3.9% year-to-year in the first quarter of 2015 compared to 5.1% in 2014. According to the

Dubai Statistical Centre (DSC) press release (16), significant growth was seen in the service sector after utilities. The service sector, including real estate and hospitality and business services, had a 5.6% year-to-year growth in the first quarter of 2015. The service sector constitutes almost 40% of the GDP in Dubai.

Although retail and wholesale trade accounts for 27% of the economy, its growth was much lower than the hospitality sector which had a growth of 9.2% year-to-year in the first quarter of 2015. Even with all the effort to diversify the economy, the manufacturing sector failed to achieve a healthy growth rate compared to 2014 but 4.1% year-to-year growth in the first quarter in 2015 did not seem bad. Still there were a number of development projects, including major construction projects underway in 2015 but relatively speaking, the growth stayed flat.

It even seemed difficult to believe, according to the Dubai NBD bank economic research report (17), as the construction sector in the entire UAE reported a growth of 7.3% in 2015. But the report continued to show confidence despite the drop in oil prices.

The report, however, notes that construction projects will continue to dominate the UAE economy in 2016 and seems positive about the economic growth of the country as well as of Dubai (18). Only time will tell if this would turn out to be true. As per the latest government sources, the GDP of the UAE stood at close to $400 Billion in 2014 which would make the GDP per capita $25,773 but $60,000 at PPP (19).

In the meantime, the government debt to GDP was just 15.68% which is trivial according to the Western standards but the Current Account had a 13.7% surplus (20). A national debt of less than 20% of the GDP can be considered sustainable.

A Blueprint for a Smart City

Dubai is one of such cities or city-states that can easy adapt and fit in to become a smart city. Smart cities are not necessarily large or megacities but self-contained and essentially wired cities that are suitable for working and living as well as sustainable in the long-run. In other words, workability, liveability, and sustainability remain crucial.

According to the Smart Cities Council, "A smart city is an urban development vision to integrate multiple information and communication technology (ICT) solutions in a secure fashion to manage a city's assets – the city's assets include, but not limited to, local department's information systems, schools, libraries, transportation systems, hospitals, power ...".

The big question, however, is whether we should plan and build a smart city from scratch as some countries have already initiated or turn an existing modern city like Dubai into a smart city. The author believes that both scenarios are possible. In the first scenario, it may seem much easier as long as adequate resources are made available and the urban planners can conceive and visualise the outcomes with clarity and purpose.

The second example is different in that the modern city with all the amenities are already there, perhaps even integrated but the future outcomes need to planned and developed carefully against the evolutionary outcomes. This is, in fact, the case of Dubai to a greater extent. A smart city is an intelligent city based on readily available information that can be processed and used to create and deliver goods and services, including public services. Today, there a number of cities in the world where some of the goods and services are provided smartly using intelligent infrastructure.

Most of these cities are adopting incrementally planned approach but others have adopted inadvertently as an emergent strategy.

Cities like Stockholm, Barcelona, Amsterdam, Helsinki, and Seoul all have adopted some form of service delivery models, whether public transit or health service provision based on the efficiency driven data-led intelligent approaches using the modern Information and Communication Technology.

In most cases, Japanese cities like Tokyo are already smart in several ways. Even in London, Oyster Card system for the payment of public transport fares is a very smart approach which has evolved into using contactless credit or debit card for payments. Along with a designated bus route and the use of Oyster Card system enables the buses to eliminate long ques and therefore shorten the journey by one-half compared to 10 years ago. In Dubai, we can see a number of elements that already fit the criteria of a smart city.

But Dubai is relatively a new city where the built environment and the infrastructure are modern in terms of world standards with some exceptions. With new constructions still underway, Dubai is said to take advantage of the emerging new technology in the design and delivery of the current projects. The use of integrated ICT system in enhancing connectivity will be expected. Both the government and the municipality are committed to operate an effective e-portal in managing the public service provisions.

Most of the public services and bill payments as well as the dissemination of public information and online applications for various public goods and services are all streamlined and carried out through e-government portals today in many Western cities. This is also true in Dubai where more than 40 different services offered by Dubai Municipality and the Government can be approached and handled through the e-government portal.

The concept of smart city stretches to several key areas. One of such areas is the infrastructure provision involving highways as well as facilities for efficient delivery of utilities, both water and drainage and electricity and gas lines. Today, we even have to install efficient telecommunication lines for data and information transmission using fibre optic network.

In an age of over-produced information and a deluge of data, speed of filtering and transmission is everything. Also, the road network and other transport and local transit network of railways, trams, and even waterways all becomes important for a smart city. It is all about inter-connectedness and connectivity.

The smart city cannot function without the external links and therefore, exit ports and accessibility to those ports, whether airports or seaports, are crucial for the barrier-free functioning of any smart city. Dubai International Airport plays a crucial role in this regard. In addition, Dubai's new Al Maktoum International Airport would add further attributes to Dubai's smart city dream.

The Dubai International Airport operated by Dubai Airports is one of the busiest airports in the world and the busiest in the Middle East. The DIA remains a hub for the national carrier Emirates Airlines and connects the African continent with Europe and Asia. The Emirates Airlines and several other leading airlines flies to more than 250 destinations from the DIA. Currently, the airport is undergoing an expansion project at a cost of $7.8 billion.

It's new and the second international airport, Al Maktoum International Airport at Dubai World Central (DWC) is operational since April 2011. The operator, Dubai Airports, has plans to expand the existing passenger terminal to accommodate 26 million passengers annually by 2017 and the construction is already underway.

When the big project of Dubai World Central is completed, the airport will have five parallel runways, with one 380-capable runway. The expansion project is expected to have a total of 24 boarding gates with over one hundred check-in counters along with and 7 baggage-reclaim carousels with a capacity to handle 240 million bags per year. It will be an ICT-led automated modern facility with all the necessary amenities. The project is part of the $32bn expansion project to create the world's largest airport with a capacity to handle 220 million passengers and 16 million tonnes of cargo per annum (21). According to the Master Plan, the Al Maktoum International airport forms the core of the project called Dubai World Central which is a140 square-km multiphase developments of clustered commercial and economic activity zones in the south of the city.

The DWC project remains region's first integrated platform connecting air, sea and land transportation. The DWC is located in the vicinity of Jebel Ali Port and Dubai Free Zone, and is designed to support Dubai's future plan in terms of economic diversification. And, no doubt, DWC will be a testimony to Dubai's effort to claim its smart city status. With this massive project of Dubai World Central, engineers are also developing a ground-breaking water drainage system for 100 years. This is a pioneering project in the region launched by the Dubai Municipality (DM) to the benefit of the urban communities close to the airport. This would protect the airport and the surrounding area from flood hazard while helping the DM save millions of dirhams annually.

The project covers 400 square kilometres and would cost Dh 2 billion. It is expected to collect and drain the rain water and surface ground water through deep tunnels to the Arabian Gulf. It is expected that the drainage would accommodate 65 tonnes of drainage water per second (22). Moreover, recently, HH Mohammed Bin Rashid also launched the Dubai Wholesale City, considered the largest wholesale hub in the world (23).

The city is linked with Jebel Ali Port and the Al Maktoum International Airport. It will be a place for hosting international exhibitions. According to the report, the project is set to take up a space of over 550 million sq. ft. at a cost of Dh30 billion over 10 years. Dubai with all its current and future development initiatives in place, including economic diversification projects, it is also focusing on the policies that would protect the environment and ensure sustainability of resources.

The overall vision of Dubai to become the smartest city is not to be forgotten. **Dubai seems to have got the foundation for a smart city with a number of features already considered smart but distinction must be made between a modern city and a smart city.**

During the last ten years, several old and developed cities in the western world have adopted and applied the advanced information and communication technology to enable them deliver some of the functions smartly. But there are new smart cities emerging too. Songdo in South Korea is one of the smartest cities that was planned and built from scratch. Here the application of modern technologies as well as the sophistication of urban planning makes Songdo really a smart city. Songdo is situated not far from one of the old hi-tech capital cities in the world, Seoul.

However, the experts still wonder whether the experimental smart city has been a success. Songdo may have the built-in rubbish sucking system where you don't need garbage trucks or rubbish bags outside the home along with other hi-tech marvels but it has failed to attract the businesses and investors who could make the city economically sustainable. Songdo is only half full in terms of its housing stock capacity and only twenty percent of the commercial spaces are occupied (24).

However, it has been an ambitious project not only for the tech-smart South Koreans but for all of the smart city dreamers. When compared with Seoul, which is already a smart city in its own right where you find the highest concentration of Wi-Fi hotspots in the world, you may begin to think which way to go for. Is it sensible and logical to build on the already existing modern cities or to plan and build from scratch?

There are several other cities already on their way to become smart although the barriers are there to tackle. Helsinki in Finland has introduced a 'mobility' ticket for commuters to purchase using apps or text message. Here, all relevant information is readily available to determine the shortest and the cheapest way to travel within the city. London already has Transport for London apps where one can find the arrival time of a specific bus at a specific bus stop and you don't need a ticket where either a debit or credit card with contactless system can be used to buy tickets. London is one of the crowded cities in the world where millions uses public transport to get around every day. The quality and efficiency of the transport system and ease of mobility of the residents remain a critical issue for cities like London or any other aspiring would-be smart cities.

Another city in Europe that leads it way to become smart is Amsterdam where there a number of smart projects are under implementation such as the City-zen project with smart grid, heat network and sustainable housing. Other projects include flexible street lighting and smart parking aps etc. Many of the smart city projects in Amsterdam are not different from other such cities.

Barcelona is already considered smart in several ways. Experts such as Boyd Cohen (25) points out a smart city should be ranked based on six key indicators: smart economy, smart environment, smart government, smart mobility, smart living, and smart people. The important thing is the inclusion of smart people which means a city cannot be smart without smart people who live in and use the city every day.

In most cases, the term 'smart' is used essentially to refer to collect, process, analyse and transmit and or present data. All smart cities employ modern technologies to do these functions using sensors, recorders, computers and monitors.

But, the term 'smart' should also encompass other areas such as the efficient and sustainable methods of generating and using energy; sustainable use of water; application of aesthetic and functional design principles in planning built environment; efficient and effective use of public spaces; and constructing state-of-the-art infrastructure and superstructure.

Finally, it is not smart without sharing information and not having connectivity. Provision of different services whether processed information or the delivery of end-user services, all requires sharing and connectivity, and the modern information and communication technologies plays an important role in the functioning of all smart cities. Barcelona has one of the efficient city transit systems although buses remain the main mode of transportation. The buses are faster, frequent, efficient, and one of the cleanest in Europe with hybrid buses. All bus shelters use solar panels to provide lighting for screens and interactive touch-screen are also being installed.

As in Amsterdam and London, Barcelona also provides bicycles for commuters and visitors encouraging people to become environmentally friendly. Also, most parking stations in the city are equipped with sensors that provide useful information such as the availability of parking spaces and other parking patterns. Drivers get real-time information through apps.

Like in Songdo, South Korea, Barcelona has been experimenting with pneumatic waste management system where subterranean vacuum pipelines suck trash below the ground and keep the city clean. In the field of recycling of rubbish, many Western cities now has bins fitted with radio frequency bar codes and Wi-Fi sensors which helps the waste management department with useful information for operation.

Songdo, built from scratch on reclaimed land is installed with sensors and high-speed fibre optic wires along with hi-tech built environment and boasts latest connectivity technology as part of the infrastructure. In Songdo, Cisco's HD telepresence system enables 14,000 residential units to interact directly with service providers (26). The ICT and tech companies love smart cities.

Singapore is another smart city-state where some of these projects have already been implemented long time ago. Even Today, the city-state remains a testing ground for several smart-city projects such as the urban digital experiment in Jurong Lake District.

The Technical University of Zurich (ETH Zurich) is operating the ETH Future Cities Laboratory in Singapore. **Professor of** information architecture at ETH, Gerhard Schmitt (27), notes that cities need to be responsive where citizens can give feedback on the running of the city to those who are a responsible.

Moreover, mobility of people and managing traffic remain critical issues in would-be smart cities like Singapore as elsewhere. Driver-less automated cars will run within the next five to ten years, at least in the smart city environment but it won't be easy to accommodate this technology in all city environments without the right infrastructure.

City-state like Dubai with its vast unused land space such as at the DWC project can easily adopt these new innovations with digital technology when buildings are designed and constructed. According to the CEO of the National Research Foundation, Professor Low Teck Seng, Singapore is trying to virtualise the whole city. They are planning to build 3D models of each building, including its internal geography so that live data collected from cameras can be used in traffic or disaster management. Dubai would definitely need such technology.

In Dubai, the roads and transport systems are managed by the Roads and Transport Authority (RTA) which is responsible for all forms of road transports, including the franchised taxis and the water transit modes such as the Abras and water taxis. Among the RTA control is the Dubai Metro network which was first launched in September 2009 at a cost of $7.6 billion is the longest driverless automated transit system in the world (28).

Dubai has one of the integrated transport systems with the application of modern technology and ICT tools to operate efficiently with safety, cleanliness, and punctuality in mind. The 75 km long metro track consisting of two lines, red and green, are planned for further expansion. The Red Line will add 15 more kilometres of track from Ibn Battuta station to the Expo 2020 site.

Some of the features of the Metro are full mobile phone coverage with Wi-Fi facilities across the network, air conditioned carriages and walkways, Automatic Train Protection (ATP) and Wayside Obstacle Detection systems in place, and front and rear cameras keep the train under constant surveillance. Moreover, it is one of the world's safest Metros with dedicated Metro Police force and some 3000 CCTV cameras in trains and stations to monitor any security infringements. The stations and the trains are fitted with Emergency Call Box and an integrated radio system between Metro and emergency services.

The RTA is determined to deliver 'disabled only' services in its systems by 2020. According to the RTA statistics (28), Dubai's public transport recorded a count of 531,350 riders in 2014 which was over 20% rise from the previous year. This accounted for a total ridership of 1.475 million daily. By 2020, the RTA also plans to further improve the bus network by covering more areas with enhanced services.

The strategy also stretches to waterways too where the water transit system will expand to include the Arabian Gulf. The RTA is also responsible for the airport taxis. The Dubai Taxi Corporation (DTC) manages a fleet of taxicabs and serves the passengers arriving at the Dubai airports. There are additional taxicabs available to serve VIPs, ladies & families, and passengers of special needs. They work round-the-clock and relatively cheaper than the franchised taxicabs. In November 2014, Dubai launched its first tram system to add additional value to the public transit system of the city. This would complete RTA's effort to offer smart mobility to residents and visitors alike. According to the RTA report (28), the share of public transport in the people mobility index in the city has gone up from 6% in 2006 to 14% in 2014 and the RTA target this share to reach 20% by 2020.

Smart lighting systems in urban environment also help reduce cost and pollution. Many cities, including Barcelona have installed LED lighting systems that optimise energy. It activates when motion is detected in addition to gathering valuable data related to nature of environment, including noise. Dubai boasts one of the largest per capita consumption of electricity in the world. Also, the use of solar energy for household water heating and lighting as well as for air conditioning can enormously save energy in a city like Dubai.

Dubai is already making enormous progress in this regard, including the use of solar panels in public and private buildings. Dubai and the Persian Gulf countries are blessed with cloud-free sunny environment and harvesting solar energy is much easier than elsewhere. Also, environment and sustainability policy is already in place in Dubai. The emirate is even considering nuclear energy as a source of renewable energy strategy along with solar power.

The Dubai Electricity and Water Authority (DEWA) has a plan called the Dubai Clean Energy Strategy which aims to provide seven percent of the total energy needs from clean energy sources by 2020 with an ambitious goal of reaching a target of twenty-five percent by 2030.

This is a gradual phase by phase process and the DEWA expects to achieve by the construction of the MBR Al Maktoum Solar Park some fifty kilometres south of the city [30]. The solar park is a project based on an Independent Power Producer (IPP) model using PV technology. In the long run, using the Concentrating Solar Power (CSP) model, the project aims to achieve 3000 MW capacity [29]. In addition to the solar park, DEWA also introduced a net metering scheme in 2015 in order to encourage the individual power users as well as the companies to install over-the-roof solar panels on a voluntary basis first and then to be made compulsory by 2030.

All in all, as part of realising the vision of the ruler of Dubai to make it the smartest city in the world, DEWA also works with the Dubai Supreme Council of Energy (DSCE). In May 2014, the DSCE launched the Demand Side Management Strategy or DSM which is part of the Dubai Integrated Energy Strategy. Confidential reports indicate that Dubai intends to save one-third of its energy and water consumptions by 2030. This to be achieved with a mix of energy supply sources, including solar and nuclear.

The DMS strategy fits well with the national agenda for promoting sustainable environment and information as well as the green growth strategy that intends to unify building codes and introduce sustainability regulations. What it meant for Dubai is to launch a new wave of growth with the coming of Expo 2020 and make the city a role model for energy efficiency and security leading to become the smartest city eventually.

Dubai as a smart city is also open for new and innovative ideas. Where else one can find a Smart Majlis (SM) or an online congress to brew up ideas and to contribute and engage in the development of a city-state? The Smart Majlis is the idea of the ruler of Dubai, HH Sheikh Mohammed bin Rashid Al Maktoum and the purpose is to invite innovative ideas and suggestions to improve and enhance the quality of public service provisions and increase the effectiveness and efficiency of the functioning of Dubai as a smart entity.

The SM invites any valuable comments and innovative ideas from anyone from anywhere. The contributors can visit the website of the SM (www.mbrmajlis.ae) and can freely post their ideas and comments under several designated categories. In fact, Smart Majlis itself is a smart idea for a smart city. The SM website says that the aim is to offer opportunities for the residents as well as for the fans around the world to present innovative ideas that would contribute to further develop the city and enhance its attractiveness in various fields - a very bold idea indeed.

It is understood that the ruler of Dubai himself will directly supervise the operation of the SM which is an integrated platform connecting 30 different entities, both government and the Municipality of Dubai. The entities or the service points covered are both the government and the Municipality departments responsible for the various functions and the delivery of services, including infrastructure development, utilities and public services provision, environment, leisure and tourism, trade and commerce, and civil protection and law enforcement.

The last but not the least, the city is in the middle of implementing its Dubai 2020 Urban Master Plan which coincides with the scheduled Expo 2020. In addition to the adoption of ICT-let smart city concepts, the Master Urban Plan 2020, developed by the Dubai Municipality, calls for an integrated urban development and land use plan which incorporates the emirate of Dubai, including the offshore territories.

The plan considers the issues of environment, conservation as well as sustainability of natural and heritage resources and therefore necessary mitigating measures are taken into consideration. Moreover, the plan also considers provision for water, sanitation, and sewer and solid waste management, as well as the conservation of energy along with the exploitation of renewable energy sources.

Most importantly, the Master Plan considers the city's urban development as a process that continues beyond 2020. The plan hopes to build and grow on the existing developments but with an enhanced infrastructure provision. Therefore, economic sustainability of the city and managing social and cultural impacts as well as preserving the environment remains key considerations. In overall, Dubai is determined to grow and prosper as planned even with the emerging economic trends characterised by having uncertain financial stability globally as well as in the Emirates. Although the city as well as the UAE was able to sustain economically after the financial crisis of 2007 to 2009, the falling oil revenue is beyond expectation that will definitely hurt the implementation of the key development projects in Dubai for a foreseeable future.

The Western economies on which the oil exporting countries depends for economic growth and sustainability are also in trouble. Essentially, the Western economic hegemony is coming to an end and their economies are suffering from chronic illnesses which the author will examine in the next chapter along with the impact of global economy on the future of Dubai.

4. DUBAI AND THE EMERGING GLOBAL ECONOMIC TRENDS

The West and the Global Economic Crisis

Impacts of Globalisation

Sovereign Debt Crisis

The End of Western Economic Hegemony

The Global Economic Trends Affecting Dubai

4. DUBAI AND THE EMERGING GLOBAL ECONOMIC TRENDS

The West and the Global Economic Crisis

The market-led capitalism as seen in the developed economies of the West remained the catalyst for economic growth and prosperity for over a hundred years. During the post-war era, the concept of market economy had entered most of the Western European nations as well as Japan. But with globalisation since the eighties and, credit-led consumption boom thereafter, we have entered a new era of global economic instability.

Now we wonder if we could continue to enjoy the economic prosperity that we are endowed with, particularly when the economic hegemony of the West is threatened by unsustainable amount of national debt. Not only the Western governments were reckless in borrowing, but also the corporations undertook to expand with borrowing ruthlessly.

The post-war economic boom and prosperity also led the wage-earners to borrow and consume at unprecedented level with the commodity called credit which the capitalist bankers had invented. Unfortunately, this valuable resource of credit has been over-exploited by the governments and corporations as well as over-used by the consumers.

The consequences of reckless and unsustainable level of credit-led consumption would prove to be disastrous in the end. Managing the nation-state economy and public finances effectively remains a real challenge today when the traditional fiscal and monetary policy tools have become redundant. Gone are the days when the nation-state economies were a closed system and, today, the global economic and financial systems are intertwined and interconnected.

The financial and banking crisis in the aftermath of the global credit crunch during 2007-2008 was the beginning of the end of the business-as-usual economic environment in the West. The traditional economic thinking would require changing if the market capitalism is to survive in the developed but ageing economies.

In a developed market economy, privatization of the provision of public services is the norm. This may include even the national health services and tertiary education. It meant, the national expenditure in general expected to be lean as generally in the case of the USA and, therefore, high level of taxation, including income tax can be perceived as wasteful by the tax payers.

In most developed nations, except a few Scandinavian countries, tax rates are relatively low. This causes the public revenue that is generated mainly from taxation to shrink. Due to prolonged economic stagnation in the West, the mature economies also find it extremely difficult to generate tax revenue these days.

The unexpected shortfall in revenue is causing problems in managing to meet the public expenditure budget. However, continued provision of essential services effectively requires more funds than ever before. In the meantime, the average wage-earner is finding it difficult to meet the ends with an over-burdened taxation as most public services provision is privatized today for which the taxpayers have to pay for.

The post-crisis economic stagnation, in fact, a mild depression in the West, particularly in the UK and USA, has lasted for so long with no signs of improvement. But our political leaders and economic policy makers, including the Central Bankers haven't got a clue what must have gone wrong so badly.

They seemed to have run out of steam and opted out to printing money under the fancy banner of 'quantitative easing'. None of the textbook theories or the traditional monetary and fiscal policy tools seems to respond anymore. Deflation or negative inflation and negative interest rates as adopted by the leading Central Banks, including the ECB, is a sign of frustration among policy makers. The author is doubtful whether the extraordinary measures taken by the central banks to boost consumption and the policy packages designed to stimulate and kick start the stumbling economies by the policy makers and governments in the West could generate any beneficial effects.

Nevertheless, market-led capitalism is spreading its wings elsewhere and the so called emerging market economies are wholeheartedly embracing the model. While the pioneer nations of the West are losing the battle to retain the status quo, their hegemonic state is being questioned. Sustaining the status quo is therefore a huge challenge in the Western economies today.

The assumption that sovereign states cannot go bankrupt is a redundant theory and we cannot go back to the good old days of closed economies of the earlier days either. Whether we like it or not, globalisation is to stay and the disruptive innovations and advanced technologies such as robotic manufacturing will bring us more challenges in the future. It would take years before the ageing economies of the West retire and adopt new unorthodox models to face the challenges of marching market-led capitalism elsewhere. The West may simply have to become parents of surrogate economies of the developing nations.

Managing the economy in a sovereign state during the crisis remains a real challenge. As a socioeconomic entity, a sovereign state is a complex organisation. We simply cannot manage such a complex entity as we manage large multinational companies.

One crucial element is the management of the economy of the nation-state. Unfortunately, this responsibility lies in the hands of our elected politicians who have vested interest in optimizing the benefits of a selected group of stakeholders. Governing a nation-state is therefore different from managing its economy which is only one aspect of public policy making.

We may therefore quickly opine that managing a multinational company is not the same as elected leaders governing a country. Not meeting the tax-payers' expectations effectively may not be the same as partially satisfying the shareholders' expectations in a commercial organisation. In a nation-state, whether the citizens are satisfied or not, the country would survive. In a commercial organization, its survival depends very much on meeting the expectation of the shareholders.

Nevertheless, managing the economy of a nation-state is not entirely different from managing a commercial organisation. In the lower end of the hierarchy, it is all about managing the production and consumption function. However, unlike in a commercial entity, the managers of the economy do not have direct control over the production. Production in a nation-state is carried out by the very same commercial entities under discussion that has direct control over the economic output. Since the state does not offer anything for sale to generate revenue, taxation and levies remain the only source of state's income.

Therefore, every democratic nation with no control or ownership on the productive assets of the country is facing the challenges of generating national revenue since it depends very much on taxation and therefore the state of the economy. This may not be true in a few monarchical states or autocratic regimes where the state ownership of the key strategic companies is common.

If the economy depends very much on certain key commodities such as oil which generates huge revenue for the state through ownership, then the issues of generating national income through taxation may not arise. Managing the public finances and the economy of a nation-state therefore requires a realistic plan with vision and goals as well as effective strategies to achieve them. This also requires us to scan and understand the wider global environment in which we live. The global economic system is complex where every nation-state economy is a subsystem. The nation-state economies are no longer closed entities and are exposed to the battering of the global economic system which is increasingly become volatile and less predictable.

Impacts of Globalisation

Globalisation with an open and interlinked global economy remains one of the key causes of this emerging reality. In the past, during last hundred or more years, the study of macroeconomic has been made a science with economists and academics churning out mathematical models to predict the economic behaviour and outputs.

Unfortunately, they seemed far removed from the reality. Econometric models for predicting the future economic events can only work when the assumptions they make are realistic and, it is difficult to rationalize human behaviour which remains a key variable in any such models. It very much resembles the astrologists in the earlier days who were also mathematicians trying to predict the future of individuals.

There is nothing wrong with mathematics but the question is whether the planetary dynamics have any influence on human traits or behaviour. In addition, even the textbook economic theories of the last century and the traditional tools of economic management do not seem to respond effectively today. The economists and the policy makers are taking it for granted that the traditional monetary and fiscal policy tools such as the interest rate and quantitative easing and even clever taxation would do wonders. With globalisation and interconnectedness through the ever-advancing digital technology, use of these tools and manipulations do not seem to work any longer.

It is obvious that market-led capitalism remained the key catalyst for globalisation. Globalisation can be defined as a process rather than a concept but it also means a philosophy based on market-led capitalism. The impacts of globalisation are severe as we witness today. It is fair to say that some have benefited from globalisation while others have been affected badly. More than individuals, nation-state economies have seen the impacts severely. For most developed economies, it has brought about misery in the long-run by taking the manufacturing jobs away from home to developing nations. With globalisation, the nature, structure, and characteristics of the global business and economic environment have changed dramatically within the last twenty-five years.

One major challenge for the nation-states is to manage the economy along with public finances when the entire world is adopting market-led capitalism under globalisation. Ultimately, it is the national economy that is under threat due to the changing and unpredictable nature of the global economy and the operating behaviour of the multinationals. For the policy makers and elected leaders, what matters is the performance and stability of the national economy.

However, given the turbulent and volatile nature of the global environment on which the elected officials and policy makers have no control, can we really find any effective answer to the consequences of globalisation? Central Bankers, economists and policy makers in the West have been trying to find a way out since the economic crisis that started some eight years ago.

In the aftermath of the economic crisis that started in 2008 with the credit crunch, developed economies, including Japan have been trying all the textbooks tools and models to regain their positions. These included even Keynesian approach of spend and grow during the recessionary periods. Quantitative easing had become the saviour and the USA has been printing money to the tune of over $3.5 trillion during the hard time. The European Central Bank remains the last in the West to do so in 2015.

In reality, the maturing economies of the West have been ageing with chronic illness unfortunately. It puts a pressure when it comes to managing their finances. The national revenue is not adequate enough to match the public expenditure budget and the challenges are to boost the national income. It is difficult to find a developed economy with a surplus current budget today, except perhaps, Germany due to its dominance over the struggling Eurozone economies.

In fact, the fiscal deficit level in the West is not any different from most of the poor developing economies. Most of the emerging market economies, including China may have a fiscal surplus and some economies would manage to have a fiscal deficit of 3% of the GDP or less. In the meantime, most Western nations have exceeded the threshold level and may have reached even a level of 7% or above. The current fiscal deficit in Britain may seem appropriate but stayed as unhealthy with a 10% deficit in 2012-2013 which was the same as the economically crippled Greece during the same period. You may wonder why the national revenue in the developed economies is diminishing continuously compared to their public expenditure.

Obviously, one key factor is unprecedented growth in pension and other welfare spending. When the economy slacks, not only tax revenue reduces but also welfare handout such as unemployment benefits payment increases. Also, long life expectancy among the retirees is another burden on the public purse. Legal loopholes encouraging the wealthy and the corporate sector to avoid tax payments using offshore tax heavens as well as ineffective and inefficient tax collection process are also causing the national revenue to decrease.

Moreover, growth in military related expenditure further aggravates the situation. And, lastly, when the economy continues to stagnate, the interest payment on the ballooning national debt also takes up a huge chunk from the current budget. When the state overspends from borrowing extensively, it can deplete the value of the national currency gradually. Manipulation of the interest rate to either accelerate or decelerate the economic growth could even generate negative consequences. The current interest rates in the developed economies are historic low but the economy seems immune to such changes. We have already seen negative interest rate in some of the developed nations with no sign of improvement in their economies. The recent US move to raise the interest rate since the financial crisis proved to be ineffective and the Fed may even consider reverse it.

Sovereign Debt Crisis

The ballooning sovereign debt is a serious problem in most countries. In the past, countries did pile up their national debts when the economy crumbled after expensive wars and during the period of prolonged recession or due to market failure. The institutionalization of the US Dollar as the global reserve currency after the war and the abandonment of the Gold Standard in the 1970s gave the USA its economic supremacy with no accountability to anyone on how the US managed its finances and the economy.

In the modern days, excessive state borrowing started with the USA who took advantage of its economic supremacy and went on a binge-spending leading to recklessly piling up its sovereign debt ever since. The credit crunch of 2007-2008 and the prolonged economic crisis that followed in the West affected several nations globally and several economies almost went bust. The sovereign debt crisis in the euro-zone economies in particular suffered a lot. Portugal, Ireland, Spain, and Greece were all rescued by the ECB and the IMF since 2010.

In most developed economies, sovereign debt level has been soaring and reaching an average of over 80% of the GDP. In Japan and some of the EU member countries such as Italy and Greece, the national debt level has been in excess of 120% of the GDP. According to the Eurostat (30) figures, all troubled economies of the EU such as Portugal, Spain, Ireland, Italy, and Greece had an average of 130% in 2012-13 while Greece holding a sovereign debt rate of 175% of the GDP.

The author estimates that the global total of sovereign debt to GDP to be over 55% with a global debt of over $40 trillion while the global GDP is estimated to be $70 trillion in 2014. The USA is said to carry a sovereign debt of over $19 trillion today while its economic output as measured in GDP is estimated to be less than $19 trillion. The US sovereign debt is almost 100% of the GDP.

With the Wall Street bailout to the tune of $4.6 trillion since 2009, the US sovereign debt had been rising still further. The post-crisis period had seen the US national debt exceeding 120% of the GDP in February 2014. This is a worrying sign as it was first time the debt level has risen over 100% since the Second World War. The real public debt can be even higher than the official figures. Some argue that it can be in excess of $25 trillion when future payment obligations are included.

The US economy is also suffering from a widening current budget deficit since the crisis reaching nearly 10% of the GDP in 2009, highest since the war periods of 1919 (17%) and 1945 (24%). The Congressional Budget Office (31) is hopeful that it can be brought down to 3% in 2015-16. But with the expected rise in the interest rate along with the negative consequences of quantitative easing, it is doubtful whether such a target could have been realistic. In any case, any recovery or improvement that derives from further borrowing and therefore adding to the existing level of sovereign debt would further aggravate the situation.

The prevailing economic stagnation in the West, even after eight years, has essentially brought an end to the boom and bust theory. Some would wonder how long the western economy could survive before it collapses. But the economy in the West is chronically ill and the decline is a slow process rather than a sudden collapse unless the US dollar collapses overnight. Rejuvenation of the western economic hegemony depends very much on reducing the sovereign debt.

Other policy measures whatever the politicians mutter come second. Some would try to manage the problem with prudent budgetary management along with such measures as austerity but may have impact on the quality in public services provision. As for abating the current sovereign debt, there is no any viable long term strategy on the table. But it remains an urgent matter with high priority that the current economic system built on borrowed money or an unsustainable level of debt finds a new but proven model in order to salvage the Western economy.

One route to lessen the sovereign debt level is to commoditise the economic potentials of the nation-state and create sovereign or national equity (explained below) to generate revenue rather than succumbed to the current debt-financed model. Even after seven years when the economic crisis was at its climax, the economies in the West do not seem to show any compelling sign of growth.

The financial crisis was just a symptom of chronic illness and even in the absence of the crisis, the developed market economies wouldn't have got the energy to grow any further. They seemed to have attained the so called saturation point or maturity stage in their lifecycle.

The low average GDP growth rate of 2% or less of the mature economies during the last decade justifies this argument. Moreover, globalisation with manufacturing sector moving to the surrogate economies from the West further accelerates the decline of the developed world. Advancing technology and the spread of the market-led capitalism worldwide will continue to influence the process and speed of globalisation. Widespread application of digital technology worldwide, poor economies seeking development opportunities and economic prosperity, skyrocketing manufacturing cost in the West, and the transnational companies seeking competitive advantage by relocating their production units to developing countries are some of the critical factors that we need to pay attention to.

While credit-led consumption has been reaching record high level in the West during the late eighties and nineties, globalisation was also spreading like wildfire. Consumer lending fuelled by the insatiable demand for consumption in the market-led economies boosted the consumption even high. In fact, excessive consumption was to become the way of life in the 1980s and 1990s. The consumers learned to borrow and spend beyond their means. Consumer credit, an invention of the capitalist bankers has exploded in the West.

The West was loaded with free money that came from the emerging market economies as investment which the businesses and consumer could borrow with ease. In the meantime, for multinational companies, there was an advantage in borrowing locally while stashing their profits offshore in order to avoid tax payments.

Nevertheless, most countries consider high level of national debt as having no impact on the economy. Smooth functioning of an economy, however, requires us to manage the national debt level and the current fiscal deficit along with its current account effectively. The elected officials and the policy makers would be making a huge mistake if they continue to ignore the negative impact of a high debt economy.

Stagnating economy with prolonged recession in the aftermath of the crisis has been destabilising the western economies up until today. We can simply blame the failing banking system in the West saying the banks were having a freeride with excessive consumer and corporate lending and ended with toxic assets. But it was more than just a banking failure.

It is fair to say that financial system in the West, particularly in the US and UK, has created an illusionary wealth with excessive consumer lending and mortgages enabled by regulatory deficiencies arising from financial deregulations in the 1990s. By re-packaging the consumer debt and mortgage papers as marketable assets and sold as financial products for investors, and enabling further lending based on the newly created asset portfolios, have led to creating the so called toxic asset.

Moreover, oversupply of housing stocks and its sales through subprime mortgages to unaffordable buyers have caused the first tremor of US credit crunch in 2007.

However, the economic stagnation that followed the credit crunch and later the banking crisis is not yet over. The sovereign debt ratio in the West has reached wartime highs. Raising the money supply through lending remained the only viable strategy. Printing money through 'quantitative easing' to buy back assets was another option that the US and UK have already tried in 2009.

The average consumer in the West is finding difficult to manage their daily expenses, including monthly rent or mortgage payments. Families with children would wonder whether to spend on food or rent and, some are said to be turning to food banks even in 2014. The total household borrowing, including the outstanding mortgage debt in Britain had reached £1 trillion mark in 2007 which was the size of the GDP. No wonder the personal bankruptcy rate in the West was also remained all time high during the crisis period. The current crisis warns us how badly the credit-led market economy in the West could go wrong.

It is estimated that the global financial system may have written-off some $2.5 trillion in debt as not recoverable. Number of major banks and financial institutions in the US had sought protection from creditors using the bankruptcy and receivership laws. At least three major banks were bailed out by the UK government during the same period. The total bailout package in the UK would have exceeded £1trillion if the cost of administration were to be included.

The financial markets, however, have improved by 2014s in the USA and UK. But, the real situation seems less than satisfactory and seems a long way from full recovery even in 2016. The market behaviour is difficult to explain when everything the policy makers and the Central Banks have tried failed to stimulate the real economy. It gives a sense of a 'faux economy' with so much of uncertainty.

The Eurozone has seen the worst during the years of crisis, particularly between 2011 and 2012. One Eurozone member country, Greece, was in the verge of bankruptcy but euro managed to hang on with Germany's blessing. While the reserve currency US dollar is having a freeride as the world reserve currency, its hegemonic state is in question.

The West may see the global economy as in trouble but the Chinese and the emerging markets see it differently. China has already overtaken the US in terms of the GDP as measured by Purchasing Power Parity or PPP which is an international comparative tool that the World Bank uses to measure GDP (32).

The emerging market economies such as China, India, Brazil, and Russia along with countries like Turkey, South Korea, Malaysia, Nigeria, and even Mexico and Indonesia were growing at an average rate of 5 to 6 percent during the crisis period where as the developed OECD countries, including the West were growing at a rate of less than 2%. Meanwhile, the emerging economies that had adopted the market-led capitalism seems to do wonders but not without the challenge of sustaining growth without the adverse impacts which the pioneers had to suffer such as the growing income gap and social polarisation.

End of Western Economic Hegemony

Today, the welfare states in the West such as Britain lack resources to deliver public services effectively and adequately. The national Treasury is empty and in the US and UK, they are running on their wheels with a relatively large fiscal deficit (reserves are excluded). With a huge national debt of nearly $19 trillion in the USA, some even estimate that the Treasury would need another $90 trillion for unfunded social security and other programs such as the Medicare in the future.

In 2012, the former chairman of the US Securities and Exchange Commission estimated it to be $86.6 trillion (33). Today, there is a sense of frustration and uneasiness among the middleclass which stands as an evidence of structural slowdown in the US system.

Similarly, Japan has seen such structural slowdown much earlier with decades of deflation and zeroing interest rate. The Japanese debt to GDP ratio is one of the highest in the world with 217% although the country is also a leading international lender. Japan also has one of the largest retired population and in a couple of decades one-third of the total population could reach the retirement age.

Similar pattern arises in the rest of the developed economies, including Britain. The pension scheme based on the National Insurance contribution in Britain and other developed economies are also in trouble. It is difficult to foresee what would happen to the retirees when the Ponzi-style pension scheme was to collapse any time soon. It is time bomb waiting to explode.

Some observers in the US say that evidence of decline of the economy is everywhere. Post-crisis data shows that half of US workers earn less than $500 a week or just $25,000 annually where the majority lives by paycheque by paycheque (34). The middle class is shrinking and the majority is aligning with the poor where some 48 million Americans living on food stamps which the federal food benefit scheme.

Moreover, the average household mortgage debt stood at $149,782 and the outstanding credit card debt was $15,422 in the 2012-13. The total student debt outstanding was over $1 trillion with an average student debt of $34,703 in the same period. In addition, the average unemployment rate and the debt delinquency among the millennials or the younger generation is much higher. Some are even said to leave the country for good with a huge debt burden on their shoulder.

The current love affair with Trump for Republican presidential nomination explains the frustration that the American voters experience with the prevailing economic situation in the country. It does seem like the end of American Dream for many and particularly for the millennials.

As for the future of the millennials, Amy Hoak in WSJ (35) points out that they are in real trouble without being able to find a decent job but carrying a huge amount of debt. The unemployment rate among millennials is estimated to be over 10%. In addition to the student loan debt, millennials are also said to carry an average of $23,332 as credit card debt.

It is also interesting to note that housing plays an important part in economic recovery in most parts of the USA. But the new generation of millennials finds it difficult buy houses because of affordability as well as poor credit history affected by credit delinquency. Some even call the millennials the 'lost generation' and for them the American Dream is coming to an end.

The economic hegemony of the US is also linked to dollar primacy. The US currency is still considered powerful although its real value has been depreciating for decades. For over 70 years since, dollar played an important role as the only reserve currency in facilitating the international trade.

But the introduction of euro as an alternative reserve currency and the growth of China as the world's leading exporter changed the situation. China has also been pursuing a currency swap strategy with a number of trading economies since 2009. This enabled some currencies to exchange the Chinese yuan for local currency. Today, there are several countries participating in this project, including the EU and UK as well as Australia, Malaysia, South Korea, and New Zealand.

In the meantime, China also is promoting the use of SDR (Special Drawing Right) as the world reserve currency but, in fact, it is not a currency in its own right. However, SDR could become one if we make it as a virtual currency as the author has proposed the concept in his previous book titled 'Global Economic and Public Policy Framework' (36). According to this concept, the virtual currency, whether SDR or not, can remain the virtual gold standard as the author suggested.

American economic malaise is not difficult to understand when one analyses the works on economic growth of Robert Gordon. He asserts the growth is coming to an end (37) and his conclusion is in agreement with the author's assertion that the hegemonic lifecycle of the West has reached its peak and is heading a decline. Gordon notes that the adverse demographics with related issues such as the cost of pension and health care, diminishing level of education in the US, unsustainable level of sovereign and consumer debt, and the negative impacts of globalisation are to blame for the declining growth.

Individual income and the standard of living in the West have been growing at an unprecedented rate since the war up until the pre-crisis period of 2006 fueled by freely available consumer credit. In this sense, the economic prosperity that the West has been enjoying seems farcical. If the status quo in terms of the standard of living cannot be sustained, the current level of prosperity would turn out to be nothing but superficial. It seems like an extremely difficult task to do so.

The economic stagnation in the West is not, in fact, a prolonged recession as it is painted by the economists and politicians but it is a sign of an ageing economy coupled with chronic economic illness. It seems like an American export but, today, it is not entirely an American problem. It may or may not have spilled over to the global system, but the prevailing economic crisis in the West is the beginning of the end of the western economic hegemony.

In fact, Japan was the first to experience the effects of the crisis even before it happened in the USA. Japanese economy, decades ago, had gone through a purge with zeroing interest rate and a good dose of quantitative easing. Japanese economy continues with the same medication even today. Since the banking crisis and the stagnation that followed, the world largest economy is still in paralysis. The US sovereign debt is nearing $20 trillion and time to time the executive arm and the legislative arm of the US government quarrel over raising the debt ceiling still further enabling the Treasury to borrow more to meet the current expenditure.

China in the meantime is said to take over the USA as the largest economy in the world soon which would make the Chinese currency de factor reserve currency. This will further undermine the state of the US dollar. Whatever the Fed and the Central Banks of the West and Japan would take to revitalize their economies are nothing more than the usual measures such as the stimulus packages that have been already tried out.

All measures are finally led to spur consumer spending which is based on further borrowing. The measures such as quantitative easing or printing money do not seem to trickle down to consumer spending anyway.

The interest rates in the West are in historic lows and there is no incentive for savers but cheap lending. Also, the gilt or treasury bills no longer attract investors either making the governments unable to fund any development projects or even public spending. Business and consumer lending, the staple of the banks, has been shrinking since the post-crisis purge. Even with state incentives provided, the banks are reluctant to lend and are cautious about unnecessarily taking risk. Many wonder excessive and aggressive lending would trigger another banking crisis.

It is the overall consensus that the credit-driven consumption and debt-led public expenditure in the West did, in fact, lead to the current predicament. The author believes that the consumers in the West should learn to consume sustainably that would require adjustment in lifestyle and re-alignment in spending habits.

In the US, it may already be happening and there is a gradual shift in the consumption pattern. However, there is no guarantee that it can be sustained and any sign of recovery can trigger credit-led consumption once again. With all the state incentives when the banks begin to lend to consumers as in the old days, businesses and consumers can go credit-craze once again.

In conclusion, it seems obvious that the West is heading towards the end of its economic hegemony, a sort of 'end of history' but not as what Francis Fukuyama (38) would have thought. The end of economic hegemony is also the end of Western hegemony itself. But it is not the end of market-led capitalism which is spreading its wings elsewhere.

However, for some in the West, it may seem like the end of an era for capitalism in general. The ageing economies, demographic shift with growing retirees along with growth in pension deficit, and the unsustainable level of sovereign debt would make the politicians and policy makers wonder if and when a workable strategy could be formulated. It is a real challenge for the people in the West and the new century would bring us unpleasant surprises. This pushes us in the West to think out-of-the-box and with vision and innovation if we wish to sustain the standard of living and to improve the deficient and deteriorating public service system.

The Global Economic Trends Affecting Dubai

Dubai's economic boom is said to have reached its peak just before the global of financial crisis in the 2007s. But during the crisis that followed in the aftermath of the credit crunch and banking crisis in the late 2007, the emirate of Dubai even needed help from its neighbour Abu Dhabi to settle the state-owned company's debts in 2009 in 2009. Since 2013, however, Dubai has managed to restore it position and the bounce back strategy had worked. With an economic diversification strategy, it was projected to grow by 5% in 2015. With all the global economic glooms, 2015 has been a good year for Dubai. Since the crash of 2009, the city state has come a long way in boosting its economy and the GDP has been rising gradually. Dubai has a diversified economy compared to some 10 years ago and its dependence on oil is relatively insignificant today.

The UAE economy as a whole has been growing during 2015 even with the falling oil prices and with the help of the government funds, economic diversification strategy and infrastructure development have given a boost to every economic sector in the nation, including in Dubai. However, the sceptics have reasons to worry. After the crash in property prices during the crisis, it has been again getting out of control particularly due to the continuing development projects that are currently underway.

The good news is however the success of its economic diversification strategy. Dubai does not depend on its oil revenue and hardly any oil reserves are left. Oil and gas output represented merely four per cent of the GDP of Dubai. According to the Dubai Statistical reports, the service sector as a whole, including tourism and hospitality accounts for nearly 40% of the GDP output in Dubai. Both wholesale and retail trade comes next which makes up nearly 27% of the GDP output. Among the service sector, travel and transportation, including aviation is in upbeat. This sector is said to account for nearly one-third of Dubai's GDP by 2020.

Dubai's main airport is already one of the busiest in the world in terms of visitor traffic. With the new Al Maktoum International Airport operating to full capacity in 2022, Dubai should become the regional transport and a trading hub with one of the busiest airport serving 70m travellers annually and the region's largest port of Jebel Ali playing a significant role in the service economy. Dubai has over 20 so called 'free-zones' where foreign companies can operate with hundred percent ownership and tax-free status. More than 1000 companies (39) are said to operate in the free-zones today. Dubai today is one of the most networked and integrated economy in the Gulf with trade, tourism, hospitality, financial services, aviation, and property as well as construction sectors contributing over 80% of the GDP.

In the meantime, Dubai is already a crowded place to live and this makes a little bit uncomfortable for the expatriate workforce when it comes to finding accommodation. The government has apparently taken measures to cool down the property market and this also have some effects on the housing prices. Also, the falling oil price has technically slowed down the economy to some extent since the late 2015.

During the time of crisis, the Government-Related Entities (GREs) or companies with unsustainable level of debts almost bankrupted the economy in 2009. Today, debts have been settled mainly by restructuring. According to Khaleej Times, Local UAE investors still see Dubai as a haven and confidence is running high although its sovereign papers such as sukuk and bonds lacks transparency. Due to the network of companies under GRE, it seems difficult to assess how much public sector debts the state-owned companies carry. Even IMF warned recently as August 2015 (40) that the emirate was loading up its debts once again. Dubai's population is estimated to be over 3 million in 2020 and 85% of them are expatriates, mainly from South Asia. However, lack of long-term commitment by the expats due to their immigration status is also causing problem. Permanent resident status such as the Green Card or citizenship for long-term residents who have worked all their life in Dubai is difficult to come by.

However, in addition to the Indians who have economic interests in Dubai, Chinese are also making investment and using it as a base for Middle-eastern and African business ventures. Strong Iranian presence in Dubai is also considered beneficial for investment, particularly when the economic sanctions are lifted. Although the government is cautious about unexpected economic bubbles, it seems difficult for the Emirate to avoid fancy and extravagant projects.

Writing about the GCC countries in the Khaleej Times (41), Khalid raises six issues supported by his research. He is convinced that that the GCC's market-stress for credit and property will escalate in 2016. His first point is the overall poor market performance in the states of the GCC that led the Standard and Poor to downgrade the sovereign credit rating in a few countries, including Saudi Arabia.

This is marked by low volume of new sovereign sukuk or debt issuance which is at 50 per cent lower, flat regional IPO market, falling almost 50% on the value of bank shares from their peaks and doubling of the cost of borrowing compared to the Libor rates.

The second point is the projected 20% fall in the sales price of Emaar and Damac Properties; two master developers, one with Dubai government stakes. Although the prices are not outrageously priced, Khalid thinks even with a 15% fall in price, it would not ignite sales as the market is glutted and property finance is credit rationed and doubled loan pricing spreads. Moreover, across the GCC States, there is evidence that 20-30% fall in retail sales, the third issue he points out.

The fourth point is the credit squeeze where the banks will cut credit facilities granted to the small scale developers who cannot match the incentives given by large scale developers. He is also sceptical about the luxury villa segment of the property market. Expected home deliveries of nearly 30,000 in 2016 addition to another 14,000 in 2015 as well as one million square feet of new office space in 2016 according to Asteco data when the market is already glutted, also alarmed him, he says. The current office vacancy rate is 40%. Finally, Khalid thinks the spiralling service charge by the property owners further aggravates the situation which discourages new buyers.

Khalid is not mincing his words when he says that 2016 will see seismic changes in property finance and bottom lines of developers as well as homeowner/investor psychology in the country. And Dubai would hit a hard landing with its collection of glutted properties. In the meantime, master developers would need multibillion dollar refinancing in the near future and any difficulties in achieving the financial targets would definitely ring an alarm bell in the Gulf States, particularly in Dubai.

When the banking system is generally squeezed and the credit is tight along with crash in oil revenue further tightens the public spending, the signs of stagnation and gloom are everywhere in the Gulf States. The construction sector in Dubai still seems upbeat with the ongoing projects as well as the Expo 2020 initiatives. Dubai is still full of major projects and some are aimed at completing before the scheduled Expo 2020 event. The Bluewater Island project, Dubai Canal Project and Dubai Creek Project along with the Dubai Metro extension project are some of these projects with a projected investment of over $2 billion.

Surprisingly, however, the entire construction sector in Dubai seems less than expected performance given the overall construction sector growth of 7% in the UAE. Even in the early 2016s, developers in Dubai seem to continue with their ongoing construction projects although the property prices are expected to fall despite the memories of the global financial crisis eight years ago still haunting. The authorities in the emirate of Dubai, however, believe that proper measures are in place with tighter regulations to withstand unexpected events and impacts as well as being able to monitor and foresee any such events in advance. But, according to Reuters (42), some still seem worried whether all planned projects could be funded amid the falling oil price and shortfall in revenue.

Property prices in Dubai have been shaky since the financial crisis of the 2008s and industry consultants Cluttons as quoted in Reuters notes that the prices fell 50% since the peak just before the crisis to be repeated again in the early 2010s. There is a sense of cautiousness in the market that it could repeat again in the 2016s or 2017s.

The falling oil price has had an impact on the finances of most oil producing countries and the Gulf States were no exception. Issac John reports (43) that, according to M R Raghu, Head of Research at Markaz, the GCC governments are expected to borrow between $285 and $390 billion cumulatively via bond issues through 2020.

The GCC's financial obligations amount to $151.3 billion this year, as quoted by a leading expert. John points out that about 52% of the funding needs for 2016 expected to derive from GCC reserves and the rest ($57.7) from domestic and international bond issuances and loans (10%). According to Raghu, John notes that the GCC States could face a fiscal deficit of $160 billion in 2015-2016 due to the slipping oil price. **Dubai's economy has effectively escaped the effects of plummeting oil prices in 2015 but 2016 would be another story.**

Fortunately, though, oil price seemed to have bounced back by mid-2016 but reaching all time high of over $100 in the near future would be a dream. Based on the expected GDP growth rate of 4 to 5 %, author estimates the current GDP of Dubai to be just over $100 billion in the first quarter of 2016. In 2015, the current deficit and other gaps were partly met by bond issues and partly by tapping into the Sovereign Wealth Funds, and for the first time in eight years, Saudi Arabia had to issue bonds locally to raise some $26 billion, as revealed by Raghu at a conference in Kuwait. Such arrangements in the GCC countries also have caused liquidity strain in the regional banking system leading to raising the interbank rates.

Raghu observed that while most of the oil producing countries has adequate reserves to tap into, countries such as Bahrain and Oman seem to have problem which is costing more to insure the sovereign debts. Moreover, lack of transparency and clarity in policies regarding debt management in some of the countries is also causing uncertainty among the investors. This causes the spreads of Credit Default Swaps (CDS) to widen and often seen as risky. Even Saudi Arabia is said to have experienced such problem leading to affecting its sovereign debt rating.

As a result of dropping oil price, the economic growth in the Gulf States, including the UAE is expected to slip. Seetha Raman (44) reports that the UAE economy will grow at 2.6 per cent in 2016 while the fiscal deficit is estimated to be 7.5% of the GDP. Banks in the country are also cautious and not willing to lend both to small businesses and consumers. High risk lending is collateralised with premium charges.

This is causing further strains in the consumption. However, non-oil sector contribution to the UAE economy is expected to reach

80% by the end of 2021 with the help of service sectors such as banking and finance, tourism and hospitality, maritime and air transportation, and import and export along with retail and wholesale.

Dubai in the meantime is hosting the Expo 2020 and its 2016 budget for transport and infrastructure development is Dh 16.6 billion or roughly $4 billion (45). Similar allocation should continue annually for some years to come. Further, with the fuel subsidies ending and fuel price liberalised along with the introduction of VAT, the UAE should be able to maintain stability. With the UAE Vision 2021 strategy being implemented, the SME sector is getting a boost with government incentives and the government expects this sector to play an important role in the non-oil GDP contribution in 2021. Also, the UAE has signed or is in the process of signing free trade agreements with several countries, including the EFA, Singapore, Japan, China, Australia, New Zealand, India, Pakistan, Turkey and the GCC countries.

Seetha Raman further notes that with a global trade finance gap of $1.4 trillion and half of which in developing Asia, the UAE and the GCC region are in good position to take advantage of the situation. Although trade finance in the UAE and GCC is growing, there are challenges relating to the economic slowdown, high cost of compliance, tightening of liquidity and new banking rules, says Seetha Raman.

As noted earlier, the GCC States are considering to issuing sovereign debt papers to finance their fiscal deficits in 2016 using syndicated loans arranged by international banks. The Kaleej Times (46) reports that Qatar is seeking to borrow $10 billion from international debt market as well as through sovereign sukuk or Islamic sovereign bond issuance.

In the meantime, Oman is said to borrow $1 billion and Bahrain is said to have launched a $600 million, two-part bond sale. Bahrain will offer a higher yield to attract investors since its credit rating was downgraded along with Saudi Arabia and Oman. Saudi Arabia was downgraded to A- negative from A+ stable. Issac John reports that according to the estimates, the Gulf States may raise $20 billion in bond sales in 2016 which is 10 times higher than the 2015 bond sales.

The UK bank HSBC estimates that the GCC governments, financial services, and corporate borrowers need to refinance $94 billion in bonds and loans in 2016 and 2017, if the slipping oil prices continue to squeeze revenues. But it may not be easy due to several factors such as credit squeeze and rate rise as well as downgraded credit ratings of some countries. According to the bank's estimates, the fiscal and current account gaps could reach over 8% of the regional GDP.

Global crises come and go but as far as Dubai is concerned, its economy seems to show resilience. Dubai's economy contracts and re-bounces remarkably well as seen during the 2009 and in 2013-14. However, Dubai today is a well-connected and integrated economy in the world and depends very much on trade, financial services, construction and tourism for its economic stability. It is technically a service cum visitor economy today which is vulnerable to the boom and bust of the global economy, particularly in Europe, Middle-east, and Russia. Therefore, Dubai's economy is essentially required to protect itself from the turbulences in the global market place.

The property market and the stock market in Dubai are very much affected by the global economic variables such as credit cycle, European and the US market behaviours, cross border trade, the

US and European interest rates, strength of the US dollar, oil and gold prices, and many more. In addition, a weaker economy in the US and Europe badly affects the visitor economy in Dubai as well as the property market.

Moreover, oil price-hit Russia as well as the other oil-dependent economies shows lesser tendencies to spend money on trading and travelling to such destination as Dubai. Fortunately, the Emirate attracts a huge number of Indian visitors where the wealthy Indians consider Dubai to be the home away from home.

Before the credit crunch and the banking crisis that followed, British banks played an important role in the UAE's financial market. Barclays, Standard Chartered, RBS, and HSBC were all responsible for keeping the market dynamic by siphoning in foreign money into Dubai but encountered huge losses in lending to commodity and energy related ventures in Asia and Europe.

Their reckless investment strategies and expansionist policies abroad hurt them very badly. Now these banks are under regulatory pressures at home and the US, followed retrenchment strategies thereby laying-off workers everywhere, including in the UAE. Some of them even exited the UAE. The banking crisis really affected the UAE and Dubai many ways.

Today, the Dubai's banking and finance sector is still getting its fair share of attention. The Islamic finance market is also growing with the state support and the emirate is already considered a Centre for Islamic banking. However, 2016 is not expected to be a favourable year for the state's finances due to the falling oil price although there is no crisis expected in the area of sovereign debt. The property market in Dubai has, however, had a dip and should continue to show its weaknesses throughout 2016.

Even Abu Dhabi banks were under pressure in 2015 to cut down their lending levels in order to maintain the government mandated loan-to-deposit ratio after falling oil prices. In the early 2016s, the interbank lending rate more than doubled the Libor rate. Moreover, with the interest rate hike in the USA and a higher dollar are expected to have repercussion in Dubai and Abu Dhabi. There expected a credit squeeze in 2016 leading to slow growth or even a flat level of economic output.

The declining oil price, however, will have a positive impact on some economies, particularly the developing economies and some emerging markets. Chinese and Indian economies should revive and perhaps, could even attain a growth more than the projected figures. Oil price may go up but not beyond the $50 to $60 a barrel mark. With the Chinese investment in Africa growing, the continent will remain a market for the emerging economies. All these would make Dubai a little bit stable but expected growth could dwindle during the next few years to come.

The ruler of Dubai has its own vision for future. We have already examined and discussed the smart city concept and Dubai is already on its way to achieve this although there are a few obstacles it would face in terms of the overall infrastructure of the city. With the current and the future plans being implemented, the Dubai will expand to swallow the entire emirate of Dubai and developments would align with the concept of the smart city.

Technically speaking, Dubai aims to be a mix of visitor cum knowledge-led service economy where key service sectors such as finance, travel and hospitality, aviation and transport, health care, and retail trade will dominate the economy with a digital infrastructure to support operations and delivery with seamless connectivity.

Moreover, Dubai already has most of its public sector services integrated and connected via digital medium where the users can access through the Internet and mobile devices. Dubai, with its recent Open Data Law, seems to support public access to non-sensitive government information. With a strong commitment and support for innovation, Dubai is also building its needed digital infrastructure that would encourage investment as well as trade. Although the pioneer nations such as Britain are sceptical about the effectiveness of Public-Private Partnership in economic development, Dubai is considering the concept for the promotion of its digital infrastructure development.

Another new development is the recent release of the Commercial Companies Law in the UAE which is in favour of the entire nation in attracting foreign investment. However, the current political situation and the prolonged economic stagnation in Europe, Brexit and possible disintegration of the EU, and a Trump presidency in the USA are serious matters to consider when we come think about economic stability of the UAE and Dubai. Unless the Middle Eastern turns its direction to the East, the economy of the Gulf countries will have to suffer the consequences, no matter whether it is visitor or service economy that the nation like the UAE aspires to be in the next decade.

5. A BLUEPRINT FOR A DEBT-FREE SUSTAINABLE ECONOMY

Rational for a Debt-free Sustainable Economy

Sovereign Debt versus Sovereign Equity

Fiscal Policy Measures and Taxation

Sovereign Equity Fund and the Sovereign Holding Corporation

5. A BLUEPRINT FOR A DEBT-FREE SUSTAINABLE ECONOMY

Rationale for a Sustainable Debt-free Economy

In a turbulent and unpredictable global economic environment, stability of a nation-state economy becomes a difficult-to-achieve objective. After all, every nation is interconnected and so are the national economies. Dubai is one of the most interconnected places on earth today.

Moreover, worldwide acceptance and adoption of market-led capitalism along with globalisation, every nation is a consuming entity fuelled by excessive dose of consumer credit. Unfortunately, even the sovereign states and the corporations have all learned to borrow and spend in billions of dollars, if not trillions. In other words, the entire economy is debt-ridden and the continuous accumulation of the debt not only makes it unsustainable but also chronically ill.

Fortunately, the oil-rich Gulf States, including Dubai have so far escaped from such malaise. The market-led capitalism is difficult to come by without the commodity called credit which we consume recklessly and unsustainably. After all, why not consume it when it is available freely and cheap. The level of consumer debt in the West is soaring and stands at an average of one-and-a-half times the average individual income. Even Denmark with a very good standard of living and impeccable public service provision, has one of the world largest per capita consumer debt.

Consumer debts and company debts are, perhaps, explainable and understandable but many still may find it difficult to understand why are the Western governments and the Treasuries in debt and in billions, if not trillions. One good reason would be the need to sustain the level of public service provision and welfare payment, including state pension entitlements in the

West. When the economy slows down for a prolonged period of time, national revenue would decrease and encounter fiscal deficit which could accumulate if the economic situation continues to deteriorate. Even in the UAE and Dubai, consumer debt is increasing whether in the form of consumer credit or Islamic financing such as Murabaha and Mudarabah. Not to mention the Islamic bonds such as Sukuk which the government uses to finance its deficits.

In countries where sovereign wealth funds are used to operate public enterprises, it is extremely difficult to classify the corporate debts as company debts or sovereign debt. The oil-rich states of the Gulf often fall in this category. The government owned company of Dubai World is a good example to illustrate this case. **Dubai World (DW) is a conglomerate operating globally under the parent company of Dubai Holding in which the ruler of Dubai is said to holds the majority stakes.** The DW is technically an investment arm of Dubai Holding which is essentially the economic hub of Dubai itself. Its operational interests stretch from transport, logistics, rig building to investment and financial services. It also builds, owns and operates free zones and hotels. In other words, all key industrial and service sector businesses in Dubai are owned by Dubai World.

In this regards, the company owns and operates several firms with independent identities such as the Nakheel Properties, a master developer and Dubai Ports World which operates several key ports worldwide, including the P&O in the UK. As a subsidiary company of DW, Nakheel is one of the leading developers in the world and almost everything in Dubai has been developed by this Master Developer. Even Today, the company remains a key player in realising the Dubai dream. Dubai intends to create one of the best places on earth to work and live, to do business and to visit for leisure and pleasure. In this respect, Nakheel has kept it promises and continues to deliver. There are, in fact, only a handful of countries that are free from sovereign debts or with a sustainable level of debt, say less than 20% of the GDP which is the total annual economic output. In fact, in terms of outstanding national debt, developing countries and smaller economies are much better off when compared to some of the Western countries and developed economies.

For examples, the USA, the wealthiest nation in the world is carrying a sovereign debt of $19 trillion which is over the size of its GDP. The UK is said to carry a sovereign debt of £1.69 trillion, almost 80% of the GDP. The third largest economy, Japan, has a debt ratio of 217% of the GDP while the troubled European economies such as Greece and Italy has a debt ratio of over 200% and125% respectively in 2014 (30).

A country like Sweden or Norway with impeccable record of quality public services carries a sustainable level of sovereign debt which is less than 20% of the GDP. So are the GCC countries, including the UAE and Dubai which carry a debt of roughly between $160 and $200 billion or just 20% of the GDP. The UAE debt ratio of 15.68%. The level of sovereign debt will continue to grow in most of the developed economies of the West with the exception of a few countries such as the Scandinavian countries. So are the sovereign debt level of most of the oil-dependent economies, including the Gulf States, and Dubai and UAE are no exception. The GCC countries, Saudi Arabia; Bahrain; Oman; and Qatar, in particular, are already in trouble and are looking forward to raising $100 billion worth of debt-financing in 2016 (46).

Dubai is currently moving to protect its financial sector with new legislation and regulations. In the aftermath of the release of 'Panama Papers' in April and May 2016, offshore registered companies and trusts came to the limelight. Even Dubai was considered a garage for parking wealth for the rich people worldwide. In this circumstance, it is a prudent move for authorities in Dubai to consider tightening the rules and regulation and maintain the reputation. In addition to a healthy level of consumption of mainly domestically produced goods and services, it is imperative that an economy of a nation-state should operate with a sustainable level of sovereign debt.

The author believes that the sovereign debt in an economy is akin to blood pressure (BP) level in a human body where the normal or healthy level of BP is considered to be 120 over 70. Raised BP level which could trigger strokes or heart attack is indeed a cause for concern. Hypertension or raised BP is a chronic illness among many and difficult to control even with medication. As there are several causes for hypertension or raised BP, high level of sovereign debt is also caused by several factors one of which is the accumulation of fiscal deficit over a period of time due to recession or economic stagnation.

When the economy fails to grow or sustain its growth, the cost of public service provisions goes up. In order to meet the revenue gap, the Treasury will be forced to borrow. And will continue to borrow and accumulate debt when the economic slowdown prolongs or the recession continues. When the current debt piles up it contributes to the growth of sovereign debt. Here, the author compares the fiscal deficit to insulin deficiency in human body. Raised sugar level in the blood indicates lower level of insulin or its production in the system. High level of sugar is the cause of diabetes which affects millions of people worldwide.

Diabetes is the root cause of several illnesses and it also affects the functioning of body organs, including liver, heart and kidney. It is also one of the main causes of raised blood pressure. In other words, widening fiscal deficit or negative in cash-flow in an economy is a contributing factor to the incremental growth of sovereign debt as in the case of raised blood sugar level versus hypertension. Persistent and widening fiscal deficit and ballooning sovereign debt are chronic illnesses and returning to normalcy is difficult to come by when the economy is inflicted with these illnesses. And the economy needs to be under medical treatment perpetually.

Then the question is what we would consider as the sustainable level of sovereign debt. The author thinks a Sovereign Debt ratio of 10% as sustainable when the economy is in upbeat and 30% when the economy in recession. As for fiscal deficit, an average ratio of 3% of the GDP would be sustainable.

In the UAE, for example, it is estimated to be over 7% in 2016 due to the falling oil revenue which is not sustainable. As the ageing economies of the West struggle to retain their status quo in terms of their standard of living and the quality of public service provisions, the new emerging economies are enjoying their newly found prosperity.

However, market-led capitalism does have a lifecycle of its own even in the new host countries like China or India. Even small economies with market-led capitalism will prosper as long as they remain surrogate economies for the West. It meant, as long as they remain the producer economies of essentially cheaply manufactured goods and outsourced services to serve the consuming nations, these countries will prosper. However, there are two conditions; the West should continue to import and consume and the surrogate and the emerging market economies should continue to supply cheap goods and services. The question is for how long this can be true. The West is chocking with excessive consumer debt and emerging market economies are slowly becoming expensive to produce.

In addition to the problems of fiscal deficit and sovereign debt, there is another issue that affects the health of the economy. It is the problem caused by fluctuation in the current account. It is the third chronic illness. Widening gap in the balance of payment is akin to high cholesterol level in the blood. Typically, it is due to high consumption of imported goods and services. In other words, the current account deficit or a negative trade balance which is akin to high level of bad cholesterol can cause blockage in the production and consumption system. Even too much of good cholesterol or high level of current account surplus is also bad. In an economic system, production should be equal to consumption to attain equilibrium.

In-equilibrium in the system will have an effect on the economy which is characterised by having business failures, high level of unemployment and fluctuating currency value and exchange rates. The challenge is to attain equilibrium in production and consumption where the excess needs to exported and the deficiency needs to be met by imports.

Hypertension, diabetes, and cardiovascular disease make an individual chronically ill so are the mounting sovereign debt, widening fiscal deficit and a massive current account deficit which make the sovereign economy chronically ill. These three diseases are interrelated and require uninterrupted treatment and medication where prevention is however better than cure. In the end, this leads us to conclude that economic sustainability of a nation-state depends very much on the sustainable level of sovereign debt, if not totally debt-free.

Sovereign Debt versus Sovereign Equity

A nation-state as an entity is a grand and complex organisation. An economy of a nation-state itself is not an entity itself but consists of a system of production and consumption. The economic system creates goods and services in the form of resources and finished outputs as well as it processes information for consumption which is an integral part of the system. Economic potential or capability of the system and the intrinsic ability to produce and consume the resources, including goods and services as well as information, is said to have a value that the consumers are willing to assign. This economic 'potential' and capability can be commoditised to create an economic asset which is an equity that can be sold in the share market to generate capital for the nation-state plc.

We already are used to do this for individuals based on their potentials and capabilities. We may assign a value based on individuals' capability, competencies, education, health condition, assets they may possess, and age as well as maturity. The wage or salaries individuals are capable of earning, their credit score that enables them to borrow, and other monetary gains (such as the earning of an artist, actor, sport person etc.) they would enjoy ascertain that we assign a value to indicate how much an individual is worth in the market place.

Another example would be entities without any tangible assets such as the Manchester United football club or Formula 1 team selling shares in the stock market based on their ability to win. Similarly, any economic value that we assign to assets is related to its ability to produce goods and services, including valuable information as output.

Finally, we also assign economic values to goods (including manufactured products and agricultural produce) and services (including entertainment and insurance policy etc.) based on the perceived benefits they are expected to generate to the buyer or the consumer. Commoditising the production and consumption potentials of the economic system therefore makes sense.

In fact, government bonds such as Treasury Bills and Gilts are IOU papers that the states exchange to borrow money from the public is also based on the perceived value of the economic potential and capability of the national economy. However, such debt-based papers, although liabilities, are sometime referred as assets by the bankers when they sell them as investment products.

As a reward for holding these papers, state promises to pay an interest on the amount borrowed and return the invested capital when the bonds matures in a given period of time. When Treasury continues to borrow using these debt instruments and sovereign notes based on the future capability of the economy to generate income, this gets piled up to form what is the sovereign debt.

This happens when the economy fails to bounce back from recession or fail to grow adequately to generate enough tax revenue. This is in stark contrast to the equity-led revenue generation where the investor takes risk with invested capital and expects to make dividend with no guarantee whatsoever. In equity-led system, we create and sell share stocks to generate revenue as capital. But even with a state guarantee, the Treasuries have not sought or would not resort to raise capital through the sale of state-owned Treasury shares. This may have something to do with the historic evolution of the concept of money, particularly, its link to the state and the creation of the Central Bank (Bank of England in 1694).

Such models have created the link between the Treasury and Central Bank as we see today. The Central Bank such as the Bank of England then could obtain the right to print paper money which could be used by people to pay their taxes. This arrangement enabled the Bank to lend the sovereign with gold to fund the wars. Earlier times, all banks were private entities whose main function was to hold the register of transactions and therefore a record of ownership and there was no such entity as the Central Bank. And there were a number of currencies in an economic system offered by several large companies or banks. Today, a multi-currency system within a nation-state no longer exists.

Nevertheless, the creation of money in the form a single currency and its link to the state through its Central Bank and the Treasury still failed to unify the production and consumption capabilities and the functions of the nation-state economy effectively. The nation-state as an economic entity was able to create neither a national equity nor asset. They instead got hooked in to the idea of borrowing money from the public through the issue of IOU papers such as the Treasury Bills and Gilts.

Following the British model, Americans leaders then successfully managed to unify the various independent States and currencies to create one united entity called USA and one single currency called Dollar. It worked very well and created the world largest economy with the blessings of the Bretton Woods agreement in 1948 after the War when the British Pound was losing its ground as the only global reserve currency.

After the Maastricht Treaty was signed to unify the European countries in 1992, the European Union took the bold steps to establish a currency union and finally the European single currency was born in 1999. Historically, the value of money measured in terms of the national currency was linked to the amount of gold held at the Treasury. But the value of fiat or paper money what is in circulation today is assessed in terms of the relative strengths of a handful of key national currencies in terms of exchangeability and their comparative values. This however is indirectly linked to the strength of the national economy and its performance. Technically, the value of the national currency, therefore, should reflect the economic performance of the sovereign state. And the economic performance is related to the economic potential or capability. In other words, performance is highly correlated to the potential or capability. So we may argue that if we commoditise the economic potential of a sovereign state, then it should be related to the value of the national currency and, perhaps, we can even measure the value of the economy using currency's value.

However, the problem arises when the currency also becomes 'money' which is a medium of exchange and record of transaction. Supply and circulation of money in an economy therefore performs a very unique function. This is also linked to inflation that is based on the prices of goods and services which can have up and down trends.

When the supply and circulation of money increase excessively, the value of money erode substantially and affect the economy negatively. Because of the dual function of a national currency, it is difficult to consider the national currency as the value of the commoditised economic potential of the nation. This requires an alternative which the author believes is 'sovereign equity'. It can be created based on the economic potential of the nation. Sovereign equity is meant to replace sovereign debt eventually. Equity can be defined as the intrinsic value that a product, asset or even a concept holds which can be effectively exploited to raise capital or generate revenue.

Equity is an intangible commodity which can be exchanged for money or capital. It can also be swapped or exchanged for debt. Does a sovereign state have any equity or asset collectively which can be considered as having any economic values? The answer is yes. The collection of economically exploitable resources and productive assets do have a value but they are not necessarily owned by the sovereign state.

If a commercial entity or business firm with a mission to organise and engage itself to produce and offer goods or services to buyers, and sell stakes (ownership) in the company as equity shares, then the company itself is said to have a value. What we see here is the commoditisation of the company itself.

Similarly, a sovereign state has a mission but not necessarily to engage in the production of goods and services by itself. However, the state technically outsources its functions to the private sector businesses in some way to produce and offer goods and services to the stakeholders. Meanwhile, the state sometimes engages directly in the provision of public goods and services via public sector companies or organisations.

Sovereign equity is not linked to the national currency, nor their values related to each other. However, a sovereign state as an economically productive entity deemed to possess something called the sovereign asset. The author would like to call it the Gross National Asset or GNA. The GNA is the total nominal value of all economically productive assets in an economy, including land and building as well as manufacturing plants and equipment used for production. Another essential item for the sovereign entity is the liability which is normally what the state owes others and therefore comes under national debt.

When we aim to develop a model for a debt-free sovereign state, the key objective remains to be creating a debt-free sovereign economy as much as possible. Nevertheless, it would be extremely difficult for a sovereign economy to operate without debts entirely. In an open economic environment, the national economy as a component of the global economic system, uncertainty remains the root cause of all the problems, including the need to borrow funds from the market.

Therefore, it is appropriate and reasonable to determine and adopt a threshold level of sovereign debt and current fiscal deficit as benchmark level. A ratio of twenty to thirty percent of sovereign debt to GDP and a fiscal deficit of less than 3% of the GDP would be ideal in order to become sustainable and therefore to consider almost debt-free.

It is however not impossible, as the author believes, to become a totally debt-free economy. Some sovereign states do have the luxury of owning valuable commodities such as oil which every other economy in the world depends on. Export income generated by exploiting the valuable resources does provide a source of national revenue. This often happens in a few monarchical economies where the state owns the national resources. Although at the mercy of volatility and uncertainty in the global market, some nations such as the UAE do manage to survive during the time of crisis.

These states often use Sovereign Wealth Funds to manage their economies when in trouble. The Abu Dhabi Investment Authority Fund and the Norwegian Pension Fund are the world's largest sovereign wealth funds each with some $800 billion worth of assets under management. Dubai Investment Corporation is also a relatively large wealth fund with over $180 billion of assets under management. There are over 80 wealth funds in the world today and some of them are commodity-led. Saudi Arabia is currently considering to augmenting its SAMA fund after selling 5% shares of Saudi Aramco in the share market in order to diversify its revenue base from oil exports.

Moreover, recent huge investment of Saudi Wealth Fund in Uber or Singapore state funds, GIC and Temasek in Alibaba.com explains the significant role of wealth funds in the global economy. The Treasury can tap into the national investment fund such as the proposed Sovereign Equity Fund, which can help manage the public expenditure effectively along with funding strategic development initiatives.

Wealth funds are investment funds that are managed by professionals but are not sovereign equity. This is often a vehicle for stashing excess profits or income generated so that any future shortfall in revenue can be compensated in a state owned operation such as the oil and gas production. Although funds from wealth funds are used by the Treasury in some sovereign states, they don't directly belong to the state coffers. The sovereign wealth fund (SWF) is different from sovereign wealth enterprise (SWE) where the former could be subject to a strict investment mandate but the latter operates like a commercial organisation with its own rules. The SWF lacks transparency and it can hide several SWEs. For example, the Dubai Investment Corporation is a government owned wealth fund which owns the Emirates Group.

Any enterprise directly under the control of a SWF is not considered a public enterprise but a sovereign wealth enterprise. Such entities often operate as a joint-stock company with its shares trading in the stock market. In any case, sovereign wealth funds are not owned by the citizens or tax-payers. Even specific wealth funds such as pension-based investment funds belong to the contributing members.

Unfortunately, most countries in the West do not even have such an investment fund for the National Insurance or Social Security contributors. Income from these levies in the UK is normally channelled to the current revenue basket of the Treasury as the tax receipts. The US does have a Social Security Trust which is not a sovereign wealth fund.

Fiscal Policy Measures and the Role of Taxation

Sovereign debt is as old as the concept of taxation. However, proposing the idea of a debt-free sovereign state probably would raise eyebrows, not only among economists but even among politicians. Even the new concept of sustainable sovereign debt is still difficult to come by when an economy is stumbling to grow, particularly in the West. In order to generate revenue, a nation-state can only offer a product called taxation. Any fiscal deficit that may arise due to economic stagnation needs to be met with the sale of sovereign notes called Treasury bills or Gilts. This is what eventually becomes the national debt or sovereign debt. In an Islamic state, we may hear something called sukuk which is akin to a bond but with an Islamic twist. However, even in an Islamic economy in a globally connected world, it is extremely difficult to escape from the winds of Western financial system.

The commodity called the credit and the resulting debt fuels the global economy. Debt means interest payment or the cost of capital that every economy has to put up with. At the state level, even Islamic countries have to endure this cost of capital when they resort to seek funds from global financial market through syndicates of loans by international lenders.

From the previous section, we have already become familiar with the new concept of 'sovereign equity' that is derived from 'commoditizing' the economy of a sovereign state or its economic potentials. It would help to generate revenue by offering sovereign equity shares as an investment in the share market. In the meantime, however, we should be cautious of making a taxpayer-citizen an investor-customer. A satisfied customer as a stakeholder of a company may build up loyalty when seems happy with his or her purchase of goods or services although he or she does not have any allegiance to the company. Meanwhile, the taxpayer turned investor-customer will be expected to have allegiance to the sovereign state.

Moreover, a customer would always need to pay for the goods and services which are different from that of the taxpayer concept in a sovereign state. Here, citizen-customer pays tax with the expectation that the state will provide public goods and services.

Today, the stakeholder is said to pay his or her share of tax as well as pay for essential public goods and services that are provided by privatized companies. Moreover, in a market-led economy, providers often would differentiate their goods and services by diversifying the offerings. They would often target more than one specific groups of consumers based on their profile such as income and affordability.

It therefore goes against and even undermines the concept of stakeholders entirely. After all, under the stakeholder concept, we expect the state to be responsible for providing public goods and services without discrimination and irrespective of user affordability. Some segments of the society, although being stakeholders, may find it difficult to pay for the essential goods and services, but we cannot exclude them. This is also one of the basic principles of Islam.

This is where the role of taxation, and income tax in particular, becomes vital. Taxation helps redistribute income through the provision of public goods and services to some extent. But taxes such as the VAT does not discriminate anyone and levied from all, irrespective of affordability.

Moreover, in a tax-levying economy, wealthy and the businesses often try to evade tax deliberately using legal loopholes. Recent leaking of Panama Papers shows how easy it is tax avoidance and even evasion in a global economic system.

The author therefore believes that we need to rethink the entire concept of taxation. In most of the Islamic states, a tax on individual income is not levied but other forms of taxes such as the VAT may exist. In Dubai, almost 75% of the state revenue comes from fees and fines, a clever idea where the state does not need to depend on tax income amid the falling oil revenue. However, Dubai's oil revenue is negligible and the income from economic diversification seems to pay for the public services.

Nevertheless, under the proposed model, the sovereign state will have something called 'national equity' or 'sovereign shares' and national liabilities in the form of sovereign debt but still lacking 'national asset' if the nation-state is to operate like a corporation and create a national balance sheet. We have already examined the concept of GNA or Gross National Asset in the foregoing section which was first proposed in the author's previous book titled 'Global Economic and Public Policy Framework'.

The proposed strategy therefore has two parts: new fiscal policy measures and tax reform that would require us to rethink and restructure the entire concept of taxation. This would include the restructuring of income tax and corporation tax and creating a national wealth creation model such as the Sovereign Equity Contribution Scheme (SECS) and Sovereign Holding Corporation (SHC) which are discussed here in the sections to follow.

Tax reform and restructuring is however a mammoth task for a tax-levying economy such as in the West. The author has proposed a new approach to managing fiscal policy with the tax reform which the readers can refer to in his previous book titled 'Sovereign Debt Crisis and economic Sustainability'.

In an economy free from income tax like the Emirate of Dubai, it may not be necessary to levy an income tax but fine-tuning of the existing model where indirect taxation such as the Value added tax (VAT) and the fees charged for services could remain the main approach. A major part of Dubai's national revenue comes from fees and fines, a clever strategy. The proposed sovereign equity model, however, requires the state to be transparent with fiscal policy measures and any taxation.

From ancient times, different types of taxes and levies have played an important role in generating income for the rulers and regimes. The types of taxation varied from monarch to monarch and state to state and the proceeds were not always used for public expenses but to the benefit of the rulers such as waging wars against enemies. British rulers, for example, gained from land tax and levies on commodities from colonial masters in the new world, and not necessarily from trade. Today, there isn't a single country in the world without some form of tax or levies. Even economies with surplus income owing to their valuable resources and exports such as oil-rich states in the Gulf have imposed some form of indirect levies or consider introducing such levies due to falling national revenue.

A market-led democratic nation cannot provide essential and public services as well as the necessary infrastructure without tax revenue and the three common forms of taxation are tax on individual income, corporation tax and the Value Added Tax on consumption.

Because of the economic uncertainty and mismanagement or unforeseen events, however, national tax revenue does not always seem adequate to meet the public expenditure needs. This often pushes the state to borrow from the market by offering sovereign notes. In the Islamic states, including Dubai, the common form of financing the deficits or development projects are from Sukuk bonds.

The author argues that the mature and developed market-led economies of the West should consider using fiscal policy tools innovatively without burdening the middle-class tax-payers. It means the notion that tax-levies are the only source of public revenue in a sovereign state require thorough evaluation. We cannot ignore the complexity of various forms of taxation, particularly the corporation tax, and the issues of tax burden on the hardworking middle class of the society.

In a democracy, paying Income tax is synonymous with citizenship and allegiance today. However, a levy on individual income remains a subject for debate today. While the wealthy tries to avoid and evade tax payments and the poor is exempt from paying income tax, only the middle class is increasingly being squeezed which is seen as unfair and, perhaps, even unethical. Also, in addition to the income tax and corporation tax, consumption tax such as the VAT is another burden on all segments of the society. The use of VAT for generating revenue is gaining significance especially in poor nations where collecting income tax is a formidable task and remains a problem for various reasons.

As an indirect tax, the VAT provides a significant portion of the public revenue in the developing countries. In the near future, such taxes could play a vital role in generating national revenue for several oil-rich sovereign states in the Persian Gulf thereby avoiding the prospects of introducing income tax.

In the developed economies, income tax revenue remains a substantial portion of the total national revenue collected, and therefore, seems almost an obsession. The politicians therefore would love to play with income tax and electorates often like the idea of tax cuts that the politicians would promise. Some countries in Europe tend to justify their high rates of taxation by providing quality public services although the middle class is overwhelmed by tax burden. Even the prevailing VAT in most of European countries is high, reaching 25% in some EU economies. Moreover, developed economies with privatized provision of public goods and services where users would be paying for them, levying taxes for the service provision cannot be justified.

In the meantime, economists have been arguing for decades on the pros and cons of levying income tax. Many would agree that the income tax be abolished and replaced by some form of consumption tax although it would raise the equity issue. Moreover, inefficient and ineffective tax systems often invite corruption when the tax burden tends to be high. The current economic climate and the increasing tax burden would encourage people to become tax evaders and dodgers. Helping to evade and avoid paying tax is a big business in the West. Tax accountants and lawyers are as busy as ever. Individuals and companies can easily form Trust and Shell companies in tax-free destination called offshore tax havens.

The industrial revolution in the mid-1700s helped create the wage-earning society and economic prosperity. And, this remains the basis for levying income tax. In the USA, income tax was introduced in 1913 but in Britain, it was first introduced in 1797 by the then Prime Minister, William Pitt the Younger. He was concerned about the public finances after the Napoleonic wars which cost the economy enormously. Today, every market-led economy with a democratically elected regime seems to levy income tax. Lack of taxation or ineffective taxation may cause serious problems in managing the economy.

If economy happens to depend significantly on one source of commodity export for revenue such as oil, plummeting oil prices as in 2015 and 2016 would prove that even oil-rich states of the Gulf may not be able to manage their economies due to widening fiscal deficit. All oil-dependent economies, including those of the GCC have experienced problem in this regard. Venezuela is another example with enormous oil reserves but struggling to survive after the falling oil prices.

The analysis above shows that if the nation-state is to manage its economy effectively, along with the proposed sovereign equity model, the role and the tools of fiscal policy measures require to be thoroughly reviewed. The traditional tax measures and levies do not seem highly effective in a globalized and volatile economic environment. The objective of taxation rests with generating national revenue to provide quality public services and as a tool along with monetary policy for managing the national economy.

In the West, however, the Central Bank as an independent entity is responsible for monetary policy making and implementation. On the other hands, fiscal policy making is in the hands of the elected officials who are often influenced by party-political agenda. In the absence of such complications, emirates like Dubai should be in a good position to plan and use its fiscal policy tools more effectively.

As far as the first objective of taxation is concerned, it seems difficult to justify or conclude if taxation would be effective in achieving the national revenue expectations totally. It is fair to conclude that the tax carrying capacity of mature and developed economies has surpassed the threshold level. It requires us to explore other innovative techniques and strategies to generate national revenue.

The Sovereign Equity Contribution Scheme or SECS discussed earlier should prove to be effective. This scheme also would be useful for promising modern economies such as Dubai in order to achieve economic sustainability.

For the tax-dependent economies of the West most of which are chronically ill, the author proposes a set of tax reform measures ranging from abolishing the levy on individual income for low-wage earners to restructuring the VAT based on the type of retail outlets under a standardized Consumption Tax. In the place of income tax, a new tax called Wealth Equalization Tax (WET) to be levied from above-the-threshold earners. In the meantime, the cumbersome company tax is to be replaced by an easy to administer business turnover tax.

Sovereign Equity Fund and the Sovereign Holding Corporation

The proposed model is also intended to create an investment company in addition to being a sovereign equity fund where share stock will be offered to contributors of the Social Security levy and other investors. Therefore, Sovereign Equity Fund (SEF) to be administered by a new independent entity called Sovereign Holding Corporation (SHC) on behalf of the Treasury but managed by independent fund managers professionally.

The sovereign equity share stock is the same concept as the author's model of General Revenue Augmentation Share Stocks (GRASS) which was first introduced in his previous works titled 'Global Economic and Public Policy Framework' (36).

The SEF under the umbrella of the proposed sovereign entity (Sovereign Holding Corporation or SHC) call it the Sovereign

Holding Corporation of Dubai (SHCD) will be authorised to issue and offer nominal share stocks like the preferred stocks at par value to the Social Security contributors in lieu of income tax which they cannot sell until retirement. The Sovereign Holding Corporation will also be authorised to offer ordinary shares, like the common stocks, to any investor at a premium price as determined by the market. In an economy where there is income tax levied from the wage-earners, SHC share stocks can be offered to the taxpayers as Sovereign Equity Contribution instead of income tax. In other words, for a flat rate of payment as the income tax, taxpayers will be able to purchase a specific number of sovereign equity shares.

The social security or national insurance payment as well as a basic flat rate of income tax payment, if necessary, can be combined to form the proposed Sovereign Equity Contribution Scheme or SECS. However, an economy with no income tax as in the oil-rich UAE and Dubai, the SECS payment forms a flat rate contribution to purchase a specific number of allocated sovereign equity shares.

In the UAE, the current rate of Social security levy is 5% from employees and 12.5% from employers. But proceeds are earmarked for welfare and health care spending only and not necessarily as an investment for pension. In order to make this as a SECS levy, Dubai can increase the employee contribution to 15% and the employer contribution to 15% as well.

Even if a tax-levying sovereign state were to abolish the traditional income tax, its economy can still generate tax revenues from VAT and other forms of taxation, including the proposed Wealth Equalisation Tax (WET) from those who are earning above-the-threshold level of annual income. A flat rate levy on above-the-threshold income such as say £45,000 a year in Britain would be appropriate. It means, if an individual's income exceeds the threshold, he or she will pay 25 % on the excess of income above the threshold.

The SECS allows the SHC to offer adequate number of sovereign equity shares in the form of 'right issues' so that the wage-earners can contribute to the SECS on a monthly basis. However, right issue of new premium shares for other investors will be limited in order to maintain the required proportion and market stability.

Obviously, the SHC as a corporation needs to offer the investors a dividend payment annually based on the growth rate of the sovereign economy. It therefore, needs to invest the capital it raises using professional fund managers. Optimising the funds yield is therefore extremely important using a diversified portfolio of investment.

Here, the SHC under whatever name such as the Sovereign Holding Corporation of Dubai (SHCD) is to be floated in the National Stock Exchange as any other joint-stock company but would require a new legislative framework to recognise its features as different from other commercial organisations listed in the share market. The SHC should be protected from bankruptcy and the share price should not be allowed to slide below the par value or book value.

Dubai already has a sovereign wealth fund (SWF) called Dubai Investment Corporation (DIC) with over $180 billion worth of assets under management. Perhaps, DIC can be converted to become a SHC or merged with DSHC unless the government decides to keep the SWF independent.

The Emirate of Dubai is a modern city-state with a resident population of less than 3 million. The adult working population of Dubai could reach just about a million and a half. Some of them, as expatriate, may even live outside Dubai in the surrounding emirates in order to avoid expensive housing bills.

In order to implement the proposed sovereign equity concept, it is necessary to register all employed, including self-employed individuals and expatriates with the SECS authority and issue a unique number which the author believes already exists. Ideally, all emirate citizens and permanent residents over 18 years old can also be registered but can be left for a later date to make it easier.

The SECS levies should be collected by an appropriate fiscal or revenue authority of Dubai which is responsible for collecting the current Social Security contributions, taxes and fines as well as fees. This authority is said to liaise with the employers and the self-employed individuals and businesses so that employee social security contributions are collected automatically as a levy on a monthly basis when the wages and salaries are paid. The self-employed will be responsible for paying their contributions by themselves to the SECS authority. The Treasury will generate a specific number of SE shares as 'right issues' every month and distribute to the SECS Authority for placement with the Sovereign Equity Fund (SEF) in exchange for the social security contributions made.

The key objective of the SHCD and SEF is to help the state to reduce the level of sovereign debt using 'buy back' strategy with the SECS proceeds or swap for SE shares at market value. This can be carried out gradually over a specific period of time depending on the expected SHCD revenue.

The SHCD will have two other functions; effectively managing the SEF to maximise the yield and managing the budgetary allocation and distribution of the fund's proceeds to the various cost centers, including development projects as well as the retirement entitlements to pensioners. The shareholder-investors will also expect a dividend payment based on the average growth GDP growth rate for which the SHCD will be responsible.

It should be however made clear that SHCD's function and responsibility do not extend to the fiscal management or current budget which the Treasury is supposed to manage. But the Treasury can tap into the SHCD proceeds if and when necessary to meet the fiscal deficit but with the cabinet approval. Generally, tax incomes and other state revenues from fees and fines should be the sources of the current budget and public spending but SHCD can come to the rescue when the Treasury is in trouble.

Dubai can continue to boast the tax-free status on individuals' income but a reasonable rate of VAT on all non-food items, excluding the services would be appropriate. However, Dubai should avoid levying any business or corporation taxes but appropriate fees and services charges can be imposed. The current corporate tax of 55% on foreign financial institutions can be relaxed and consider taxing all financial transactions instead. Segmentation and targeting strategies for taxation and fees would prove to be very effective. A good example would be the existing occupancy tax on tourists staying in five star and luxury hotels.

With regular 'right issues' of Sovereign Equity shares against the monthly SECS contributions by the taxpayers, the size of the fund can grow much faster than expected and this would enable the entire sovereign debt to be wiped out in a short period. Moreover, excess funds can also be used to meet the fiscal spending needs or to fund new development projects so that the GDP growth can be maintained. The emirate wouldn't need to resort to issuing IOU notes, raising funds through syndicated loans or even issue Sukuk. It means, at the sovereign or Treasury level, Dubai could be hundred percent debt-free and therefore interest-free which is essentially Islamic in philosophy.

As long as the GDP growth is maintained with the help from the proceeds of the SEF, there will always be a demand for Dubai's Sovereign Equity Shares (DSES) in the financial market. For the investors, Dubai SE shares would be extremely a better option than buying sovereign debt notes or sukuk as it is guaranteed that the share price will not fall below the threshold and the shareholders will earn a dividend based on the GDP growth rate.

With funds available for government spending from the SHCD and the use of prudent fiscal policy measures such as lowering or adjustments in the SECS levy, if required to boost or constrain consumption, the state can manage and maintain a healthy GDP growth rate. This would again guarantee the investors a safe return on investment. In other words, recession could be thing of the past and impact of the global economic forces would be less.

The government of Dubai may not require any reserve funds and the sovereign wealth fund such as the Dubai Investment Corporation can be merged with the proposed Sovereign Holding Corporation of Dubai or leave it as it is. However, it is essential that the SEF is managed professionally with transparency by the proposed independent SHCD. The SEF will be free to make investment anywhere in the world that fits the Islamic principles of investment or as long as it is ethical and it complies with sharia. In the meantime, the author would like to recommend that the SEF holds reasonable stakes in the domestic strategic companies. Managing the SEF effectively will be the biggest challenge of the SHCD.

When it comes to investing the proceeds from the SEF, it should be made mandatory that at least one-third of the fund is invested in the national strategic companies. These may include both profitable private and public joint-stock companies involved in the provision of key goods and services such as defence, utilities, transportation, telecommunication, and banking and finance. In Dubai, most of the companies owned by Dubai World, Emirates Group of companies, and even the national media and telecommunication firms would fit into the categories of strategic companies. A healthy 20 to 25% stake in the above-mentioned companies would guarantee profit for the SEF as well as help maintain the public interest in the provision of strategic goods and services, including health care

Another third of the SEF proceeds could be invested in any ethical global investment opportunities such as strategic companies worldwide but carefully chosen to deliver stable and almost risk-free yields. Ambitious and fantasy project with high degree of risk should be avoided from the portfolio at all time. The remaining funds should be made available for any economic development projects with guaranteed returns within the country. The SHCD should also remain the rescue fund in the form a reserve for the Treasury. The Treasury should be able to tap into the SEF for funds when needed to meet any unexpected fiscal deficit as well as for funding projects of strategic development, including infrastructure. Any policies of funds allocation should be made transparent and accountable. Time to time, the SHCD could also lend money to the state-owned or other joint-stock companies of strategic importance using the Islamic sukuk model.

Assuming that Dubai has a workforce of 1.5 million, including the self-employed, who are earning an average of $24,000 a year, and we can expect it to yield $36 billion if we take just 10% of the total of the earnings from the SECS proceeds annually. It means an average of $200 worth of SE shares can be acquired by each individual SECS payer every month.

If the book value of the SE share is, say $1 or roughly Dh 3, it would make an allocation of 200 shares per month per SECS payer. Also, $36 billion would make roughly one-third of the annual economic output or GDP of Dubai. Here, the SEF will have an equity value of $36 billion that the SHCD has to manage along with another similar amount coming from the issue of SE shares to outside investors at a premium price. If we name the shares of SECS payers as preferred stocks and the others as common stocks, it is not recommended to let the total equity value of latter shares to exceed the total value of former shares.

However, the Treasury can allow the SECS payers to buy additional shares in excess of their rightful allocations at 'right issue' price, if necessary. This will enable the SHCD to raise an equity capital to the tune of 70 to 80% of the emirates GDP every year. And, Dubai would never need to be in debt. In Dubai, the current state-owned companies such as the Dubai World and the sovereign wealth enterprises (SWE) such as the Emirates Airlines or EMAR can continue to operate independently with government oversight. The ruler of Dubai may or may not hold any stakes in these companies where some of them are join-stock companies. Ideally, the SEF will have stakes in these companies as an institutional investor.

However, the SHCD should remain independent from these entities except holding a reasonable stake as any other key shareholder such as the investment funds or insurance companies. Since these firms are for-profit companies providing essential goods and services, SHCD could exert justifiable level of influence over the operation on behalf of the SECS payer investors who are the citizens and rightful residents of Dubai.

Glossary

Current Account: It is the annual national account showing the value of imports and exports, including flow of investment capitals and other funds from and into the country.

Fiscal Deficit: the negative balance between the annual state revenue from tax levies and public spending, including the interest payment on the outstanding sovereign debt.

GNA: The Gross National Asset which is the total gross value of all the economically productive assets in a sovereign state.

GRASS: General Revenue Augmentation Share Scheme is equivalent to the Sovereign Equity concept initially proposed by the author in his book titled 'Global Economic and Public Policy Framework' published in 2007.

GRE: Government-Related Entity is a commercial organisation owned by the government such as the Sovereign Wealth Enterprise often through its Sovereign Wealth Fund.

PPP: Purchasing Power Parity is a measure of the Gross National Product of a nation based on the purchasing power of the national currency rather than on its exchanged value to the dollar.

Quantitative Easing: A process by which the state (treasury) buys back sovereign notes such as the outstanding Treasury Bills and other debts by virtually printing money.

SECS: Social Security Contribution Scheme which is a levy on wage-earners that allow them to exchange and buy sovereign equity shares on a monthly basis.

Sovereign Debt: Long-term national debt accumulated over a period of time as a result of state borrowing using such instruments as Treasury Bills to meet the fiscal deficits and for funding strategic and development projects.

Sovereign Equity (SE): It is a concept of national equity created by commoditising the national economic potential and capability to generate intangible assets in the form of share stocks to be sold as an investment product.

SEF: Sovereign Equity Fund is the investment fund created to receive the SECS levies and invest in various but appropriate profit-generating projects and businesses.

SHC: Sovereign Holding Corporation which is an independent company under the Treasury supervision that will manage the SEF and its proceeds, including the fund's allocations.

SWE: Sovereign Wealth Enterprise which is a company or commercial enterprise owned by a SWF which is different from public sector organisations or publicly owned companies.

SWF: Sovereign Wealth Fund which is an independent investment fund maintained by the state to generate revenue in order to manage any fluctuation in income in an essentially a state-run operation.

WET: Wealth Equalisation Tax which is a new tax proposed in lieu of the traditional income tax but levied from individuals whose income exceeds a higher threshold level (say twice the national average income).

Notes:

1. Emirates247.com (ret.26 February 2016)
2. Trucial States, Destination360.com/middle-east/united-arab-emirates/history (ret.13 May 2016)
3. Ottoman Empire, Encyclopedia.com (ret.13 May 2016)
4. History of Arabian Peninsula, Destination 360.com (ret. 11 March 2016)
5. British Protectorate Treaty, www.ukinuae.fco.gov.uk
6. Modern State of Dubai as a trading hub, TEN Guide, the emiratesnetwork.com- see also 25
7. UEA budget, www.mof.gov.ae/En/budget
8. www.reuters.com/article/emirates-budget(ret.14July 2016)
9. www.gulfnews.com/news/uae/governance/legislative-body
10. www.eia.gov/beta/international/rankings/#?prodact=53-1&cy=2014
11. The Oil and Gas Journal (BP Statistical Review of World Energy, 2015)
12. The UAE GDP www.imf.org/external/datamapper/index.php
13. The US EIA, the CIA World Fact Book, www.web.archives.org
14. Maceda C (15 August 2015) UAE electricity consumption can grow 'more rapidly'
15. Dubai Airports (www.dubaiairports.com)
16. Press Release (Dubai Statistical Centre, September 2015)
17. Dubai NBD Economic Research Report, September 2015
18. Emirates NBD Research (2, September 2105)
19. www.tradingeconomics.com (ret. 2 March 2016)
20. www.ieeconomics.com 2 March 2016
21. Dubai Airports 2016 www.dubaiairports.com
22. The National UAE (23 June 2015)
23. Dubai Wholesale City, Arabianbusiness.com (rt.1 March 2016)
24. Williams, L, Tomorrow's Cities: just how smart is Songdo? BBC 3 September 2013
25. www.wired.co.uk/article/smart-city-planning-permission (11 January 2016: Venkataramanan)
26. Cohen B (@ Venkataramanan), wired.co.uk as above
27. Shmitt G (@ Venkataramanan), wired.co.uk as above

28. Dubai RTA statistics 2016 (www.rta.ae)
29. Solar Park in Dubai (Dubai Strategic Energy Authority, 2015)
30. Eurostat, 2014 (ec.europa.eu/Eurostat/web/
31. www.CBO.gov/publications/(2014/15)
32. PPP. www.oecd.org/prices-ppp
33. Stokes, B (elliottwave.com/freeupdates/archives) rt.27/11/12)
34. Saleem, N (2014) 'the End of US Hegemony' in Sovereign Debt Crisis and Economic Sustainability
35. Hoak, A (WSJ: Market Watch, May 2014), Status of the Millennials
36. Saleem, N (2011) 'Global Economic and Public Policy Framework'
37. Gordon R (NBER, 2012) 'Faltering Innovation confronts the Six Headwinds'
38. Fukuyama, F (1992) 'The End of History and the Last Man'
39. Khaleej Times (6 June 2016) more than 1000 offshore coms
40. Critchlow, A (2, August 2015) Guardian
41. Khalid, Khaleej Times (29 February 2016)
42. Reuters (9 March 2016) issues of funding the planned projects
43. John, I; Khaleej Times (20 March 2016)
44. Seetha Raman, Khaleej Times (3 April 2016)
45. Seetha Ramen, Khaleej Times (3 April 2016)
46. John, I; Khaleej Times (9 March 2016) on Borrowing and debts of GCC countries

www.ingramcontent.com/pod-product-compliance
Lightning Source LLC
Chambersburg PA
CBHW071820200526
45169CB00018B/475